THE STUPID FOOTBALLER IS DEAD

INSIGHTS INTO THE MINDSET OF A PROFESSIONAL FOOTBALLER

PAUL McVEIGH

B L O O M S B U R Y

LONDON · NEW DELHI · NEW YORK · SYDNEY

Published by Bloomsbury Publishing Plc
50 Bedford Square
London WC1B 3DP
www.bloomsbury.com

First edition 2013

Copyright © 2013 Paul McVeigh and John Carter

ISBN (print): 978-1-4081-9375-4
ISBN (ePDF): 978-1-4081-9377-8
ISBN (EPUB): 978-1-4081-9376-1

Acknowledgements
Cover photographs © Getty Images
Inside photographs featuring: Paul Scholes © Jaggat Rashidi/Shutterstock.com; Fernando Torres and Cristiano Ronaldo © Yiannis Kourtoglou/Shutterstock.com; Lionel Messi © Natursports/Shutterstock.com; Steven Gerrard © photoplanet.am/Shutterstock.com; Arsène Wenger © cjmac/Shutterstock.com; Robert Green and Scott Parker © katatonia82/Shutterstock.com; James Milner © Photo Works/Shutterstock.com; Grant Holt and Paul Lambert © Norwich City Football Club; Danny Welbeck © Nata Sha/Shutterstock.com; Colin Murdock © Press Association; Other photos featuring Paul McVeigh are the property of the author. Commissioned by Kirsty Schaper
Edited by Nick Ascroft

This book is produced using paper that is made from wood grown in managed, sustainable forests. It is natural, renewable and recyclable. The logging and manufacturing processes conform to the environmental regulations of the country of origin.

Typeset in 11pt on 14pt Minion by Saxon Graphics Ltd, Derby

Printed and bound by CPI Group (UK) Ltd, Croydon, CR0 4YY
10 9 8 7 6 5 4 3 2 1

CONTENTS

ACKNOWLEDGEMENTS

The first person I want to thank is John Carter for his support in the creation of this book. It has only happened because he has had the skill and patience to put it all together. So a huge thanks to him.

Then, going right back to the very start, my mum and dad have been more supportive than I could have ever expected, giving me the love and security to succeed in football. I feel very blessed they are my parents. My two brothers, David and Brendan, and my elder sister Laura, have also always helped and encouraged me – and there have been times when I have definitely needed them more than they'll ever know.

When I first came to England Tim and Jackie Ball pretty much adopted me as a son, and after leaving my family and friends behind in Northern Ireland that was much needed. Huge thanks to them and they are still very close friends.

Then I want to thank all my many friends. It is a cliché to say that there are too many to mention, but I am still in regular contact with 20 to 30 friends that I went to school with. Most people lose touch with a lot of their school friends, but I still see them, speak to them and go on holiday with them.

A bit left field, but I feel like I also need to thank Anthony Robbins, who is the author of the book *Awaken the Giant Within*, which Tim Ball gave me in November 1995. Tim inscribed the words 'to your success from Tim, November 95'. That was the first time my eyes opened towards personal development and developing my mindset and attitude. The book had a massive impact on me, and when I was undertaking a speaking course over in America I actually ended up staying with Anthony's son, Jairek, in an apartment. It's funny how life turns out like that.

In terms of sports psychology there are three people who have mentored me.

I used to see Dr Craig Mahoney, a qualified sports psychologist based at Roehampton University, every week when I was a young kid at Spurs. He started me on my journey.

Then when I became an established first-team player, I worked with Keith Mincher, one of the foremost sports psychologists. He had a huge impact on me and is still the most profound man I have spoken to. If you ever want to have a chat that blows your mind then Keith is the one to speak to. It shows you how good he is that he is currently Performance Analyst for the England under-21 football team.

The last one is my good friend and role model, Gavin Drake. I worked with him when he was a sports psychologist at Norwich and I was in the first team there. He helped me view my life in a different way. The reason I stopped playing football when I was 32 was to go and work with Gavin, and now I have set up a new company with him called 'ThinkPRO'.

This book would not have been written without the contributions of all of the above people – thanks to them all.

FOREWORD

Chris Hughton, Manager – Norwich City Football Club

I've now been in professional football for more than 35 years, as a player, coach and manager. In that time I've worked with many footballers of different ages, abilities and nationalities and, in my opinion, it is no surprise that Paul has made the very best of the qualities he has.

I first met Paul when I was reserve team coach at Tottenham Hotspur. He was a 16-year-old, looking to make a career for himself in the game. It was immediately clear to me that he had strong ability, and over the time that we worked together I also grew to appreciate that he was a hard worker with a really good, enthusiastic mindset.

Footballing talent, tactical awareness, technical ability and physicality are all undoubtedly important, but in my view a strong work ethic, mental resilience and a constructive attitude are crucial to help players sustain long-term careers in what is a highly competitive profession.

When Paul was a youngster at Tottenham it was understandably difficult for him to break into an extremely strong first team squad. He could have been frustrated, disheartened or demotivated, but he always put in 100 per cent effort and had an infectious smile on his face the whole time. I think he's been like that at every club he's played for; always a good influence on others in the dressing room.

Having enjoyed working with him at Tottenham, it has been a source of pleasure to me that he enjoyed a long and successful playing career and has transitioned so seamlessly into a variety of activities since he hung up his boots. This includes a wide range of media duties where his personality has endeared him to many. In addition, he is currently working with our young academy players here at Norwich City to help them develop their mental approach to the game.

So it is seems logical that he has concentrated on this area when writing this book for football fans and players. I certainly hope that all that read it enjoy and benefit from Paul's positive outlook.

INTRODUCTION

BELFAST BOY WITH 2020 VISION

In the unlikely event that my life in football is ever made into a feature film, the opening sequence will probably be seen through the eyes of the manager of a youth team in Northern Ireland. He will be running a coaching session one sunlit summer's evening, watching enthusiastic youngsters, around 11 years old, playing a practice game.

Amid the jumbled ebb and flow of the action his eyes will keep returning to the smallest boy in the group. He will be six inches shorter than the others and easily knocked off the ball by the bigger boys, but it will be clear that he has been blessed with a gift for the game. His movement is sharp and coordinated; he can control a ball without thinking and then pick out a pass to a teammate; he can find space, dribble and shoot. That helps him to stand out from the crowd, and the manager – who is also a scout for the illustrious Tottenham Hotspur Football Club in England and is seeing the boy in action for the first time – decides that here is a potential star of the future who will certainly be of interest to the club.

I guess Steven Spielberg may have different ideas on the start of the film but there is no doubt that this was a critical moment in my young life. The manager was Robbie Walker and I was the wee boy. As a result of that practice he asked me to go over the water to Spurs for some sessions, and several years later I ended up signing professional terms with them. Fortunately Robbie – who has become a good friend and is still unearthing gems for the club – spotted that I had enough raw, natural talent to give them something to work with. But there is no doubt that I was far from the 'whole package'.

Later, as my career progressed, I came to the conclusion that to be the 'whole package' as a professional footballer you need three main attributes: first, *natural ability* – the gift of coordination and sporting ball sense; second, *physicality* – speed, strength and stamina; and third, a *strong mentality* – smart thinking, having the mental resilience to cope with setbacks, being driven and dedicated enough make the most of your talent.

Rating the schoolboy version of myself against those criteria the thing that was most in my favour was the natural ability that I displayed in that practice match. When it came to physique I was at a clear disadvantage to others. I was small for my age, and even by the time I was a 14-year-old

Belfast boy at 12 years old with an array of trophies. I was fortunate to be blessed with some natural talent for the game.

I was still less than five feet tall. Yes, I was sharp and well balanced, but over more than 10 yards there were plenty of other boys who were quicker, and they were certainly much stronger and possessed greater stamina.

Mentality is the really interesting one. I am tempted to write that as a youngster I had no mental skills at all. Without doubt I had no comprehension of what *mentality* meant and like many others I didn't consciously think at all. I just played football, and everything I did, both off and on the pitch, was totally instinctive. Yet I think it would be wrong to say that there was nothing going on between my ears. It was just that I was ignorant of what it was.

My psychological mindset at that stage was largely driven by genetics – I was naturally upbeat and cheerful – and the fact that I grew up within a stone's throw of the Falls Road in West Belfast at a time of deep civil unrest and violence. It was a seriously tough place. For instance, my best friend's Dad, our next-door neighbour, got shot in the back in a tit-for-tat killing. Of course that was deeply shocking, but at the time I didn't give my environment a second thought. I knew no different. This was my version of normal, a normal where we constantly played football in the street and it was commonplace for bombs to go off in the distance, commonplace for soldiers to walk past us down the street with rifles in their hands, commonplace for vehicles to be doused in petrol, set on fire and burned out.

While I usually just observed these incidents there were times when I got sucked into the disarray, such as during a dark evening when I was out with my friends in West Belfast, near my parents' home, in an area that was often at the core of the violence. We saw buses being set on fire and word came that there was going to be a riot. I never got actively involved in the unrest, but some of my friends were keener and, ill advisedly, I followed them. We turned a street corner to find around a thousand or so activists at the top of a hill looking down at the police station, with 15 to 20 jeeps outside and a mass of soldiers.

At the top of the hill many threw petrol bombs – bottles filled with petrol and ignited by a lit rag – down at the soldiers. Eventually the soldiers responded with candle-shaped plastic bullets. People on both sides were getting injured. After a while the soldiers came at the group from all sides and it was clear that for safety's sake we needed to disperse at some speed. My fitness kicked in as I sprinted away, along with around 30 others down side roads, with the soldiers in hot pursuit. I saw a taxi in a driveway and dived under it breathlessly, my heart going at 100mph. Someone else dived into the long grass nearby. It was a dark night, but a police spotlight picked up the guy and they grabbed him, beat lumps out of him, arrested him, put him in the jeep and took him away. I was terrified, but somehow my hiding place worked and I wasn't found.

Incidents like that simply must have had an impact on my mindset, yet the ongoing conflict was just as much part of my everyday existence as eating my dinner. Indeed, when I first left the heart of Belfast and went over to Tottenham I was surprised that there were no tanks driving down the street, no soldiers and no bombs.

But what effect did being a Belfast boy have on me? I think that it helped me to have an appreciation and gratitude for the good things in life, and it undoubtedly toughened me up and gave me an inner resilience. Helped by my mum, my dad and my surroundings, I learned to stand up for myself and not be bullied. I was probably the least streetwise of my mates but comparatively battle-hardened compared to some of the mollycoddled softies in England.

Yet in my youth I was blissfully unaware of this and the kind of mental skills that would help me to play professional football successfully. If we track the progress from the 14-year-old Paul McVeigh who signed schoolboy forms with Tottenham Hotspur to the 32-year-old Paul McVeigh who finished his football career with Norwich City at the end of the 2009/2010 season, then it was in my psychological approach and attitude that I took quantum leaps forward.

Of course as a 32-year-old I still had my natural ability. That never leaves you and, for me, is impossible to teach. But all professional footballers are talented. My physique had developed to some degree. I had worked hard to develop my sprinting skills and my upper-body strength. Yet I was disadvantaged by standing only five foot six inches tall, something that several managers saw as a problem. So I don't think I could argue that my physique was an asset. No, I am absolutely convinced that what enabled me to sustain a career playing professional football for nearly 16 years, play in the Premier League, represent my country and build up an abundance of happy footballing memories was the fact that I became football smart. That was where I excelled, a view that is endorsed by the words of top manager Paul Lambert when he kindly wrote of me that 'few have been more driven and determined to make the most of their ability'.

Certainly, through a real thirst for knowledge, a desire to innovate and excellent role models I implemented tools and techniques that helped me to make the best of my ability and develop new layers of professionalism and thinking as my football career progressed. Again I am indebted to Robbie Walker, the manager of that youth team and scout for Spurs. Early on he said something that has stuck with me. He suggested that although I had talent it would be the three Ds – drive, dedication and determination – that would decide whether I had a long-term career. You need to have some natural aptitude, but even at that tender age I realised that it wouldn't be enough on its own and everything that subsequently happened in my career endorsed that. I played with players who lifted the World Cup at under-21 level with England and had an abundance of natural talent but didn't sustain a career for more than a couple of years.

In a nutshell that is why I have written this book. I want to share what I have learned. I think the attitudes and techniques have been of great benefit to me outside of football and I believe they will benefit others.

However, I want to make one point clear at the outset: I am no saint. No goody-goody. No teacher's pet. Yes, I have worked hard. Yes, I have been a positive thinker. Yes, I have exhibited all the qualities that Robbie Walker recommended, and for much of my career I was a conscientious professional. But that is not the whole story. There have been times when I have fallen from grace, big time. So within the pages that follow you'll read about when I played in a game when I was still drunk from the night before; how I partied so hard one summer that I returned to pre-season catastrophically out of shape; and how, for two years when I should have been at the peak of my career, I lived a rock star's lifestyle and became 'Macca, the nightclub regular' rather than 'Paul, good pro'.

By the way, I would argue that having these flaws, these lapses, actually made me stronger – they helped me learn and make my insights of greater value. I'm not pretending to be superhuman. I was not and am not perfect. But as much through the downs as the ups I think I have acquired knowledge that can be of great value to others. So in this book I will outline my 12 eureka moments when I learned lessons in how to think constructively. They helped me to survive and occasionally flourish in a highly competitive industry.

These lessons can be applicable to all, but they are particularly relevant for anyone who is looking to play better football – particularly at professional level – not least because of the way the game has changed since I was that 11-year-old wee boy catching the eye of the scout from Spurs.

During my career football evolved at great pace, both off and on the pitch. Off the pitch, pre-match preparation and post-match recovery became more professional and scientific. Particularly in the Premier League, many clubs supported their players with armies of specialists in areas such as hydration, nutrition and conditioning. Their guidance encouraged players to become more professional in their outlook. They got slimmer, quicker, fitter and stronger. Perhaps there were fewer characters and mavericks in the game because, as performances improved, it was no longer possible to get by on talent alone.

On the pitch football also evolved. It used to be a really physical game, with the likes of Wimbledon able to muscle and bully their way to success through use of the long ball and sheer brute force. But as time went on the passing teams dominated. Rule changes, and the increasing influence of European and South American footballers that were more inclined to fall to the ground, meant that the better defenders hardly tackled at all. They were positionally astute, read the game, stayed on their feet, intercepted and only dived in when there was no alternative.

In all positions on the field, bit by bit, the need for physical strength was superseded by technique and smart, strong thinking, allowing players such as Cesc Fàbregas, who is technically a genius but has a slight frame, to prosper.

By the end of my career I'd say that to be a successful footballer over any length of time you needed to be capable in all of the three areas – what I call 'the footballing triad' – that I outlined earlier. Natural ability, physique, mental skills – you needed them all. To play at a really high level you needed to excel in at least one, and the best of the best were outstanding in all three. In fact, by the end of my career if you didn't have a strong mentality – if you were a stupid footballer – then you couldn't sustain a long-term career. Professional football in the modern era is played every bit as much in the mind as on the pitch.

Recent research detailed by Matthew Syed in his excellent book, *Bounce*, highlights the importance of a strong mind above natural gifts and an unrelenting work ethic above raw talent. Syed uses the latest in sports science, neuroscience, psychology and economics to put forward the view that the pathway to excellence lies in hard work and the right attitude rather than genetics. It's a view that I entirely endorse – and a constructive mindset underpins this because without it the footballer will not put in the necessary hours to hone their technique. Increasingly ability is becoming seen as no more than a decent starting point.

And make no mistake; football will continue to evolve along these lines. The hard workers will prosper and on the pitch there will be no going back to Wimbledon's 'crazy gang'. Football in the year 2020 will have even less emphasis on physical strength and tackling. It will have become less of a contact sport and more about technique and speed. Fitness levels will increase and the game will become even faster. Those most likely to flourish will be athletes with fast movement, quick feet and a sharp brain.

The current Spanish international side are signposting the way ahead, showcasing how football is going to be. Recently, the team has become known for using a style of play called 'tiki-taka', which involves fluid movement and positional interchange among its talented midfielders, manoeuvring the ball around in intricate patterns using sharp, short passes.

They have a rich crop of players who largely play in these positions: Xavi, Andrés Iniesta, David Silva, David Villa, Cesc Fàbregas, Juan Mata and the like. There are some obvious similarities within this group. All are comfortable on the ball, able to see and execute a pass, play round the opposition in triangles, hold off their man, fantastically fit, quick in mind as well as body – and they don't depend on size or strength to be a world-class footballer.

And it's not just Spain. Many of the world's top exponents of the game have similar traits. Luka Modrić from Croatia, Mesut Özil from Germany, Andrea Pirlo from Italy, Samir Nasri from France, Eden Hazard from Belgium, England's Jack Wilshere and Argentina's Lionel Messi are just some of the modern-day players that come to mind.

These pass masters are all comfortable in possession, no matter where they are on the pitch and whether they are closely marked. Contrast and compare that with England and the Republic of Ireland in the 2012 European Championships. How old-fashioned did they look? The Republic were outclassed and off the pace against the better teams, and England, despite having some world-class players in their team, had very little of the ball.

Possession is king in the modern game and this was never more evident than in England's quarter-final against Italy. Italy had 75 per cent of possession, and Pirlo orchestrated the play with such assurance he might have been wearing slippers and smoking a cigar. In contrast England were unable or unwilling to pass their way through the midfield, and that wasn't just down to tactics and systems. I remember one instance that highlighted the difference in approach. Substitute Jordan Henderson played a pass back to Ashley Cole in the left-back area and ran off, away from him. Cole needed him to be available for the next short pass to play their way out, but by then Henderson had his back to him.

Of course there will always be a place in big-time football for a wide variety of physiques, characters and styles. I'm just suggesting that as the game advances, tiki-taka, as brilliantly displayed by Spain and Barcelona, will become even more prevalent at all levels. That knowledge is gold dust for a wannabe as it provides a strong indication as to what will be needed to succeed in top-class football in 2020. So my advice to a young aspirant is clear: get used to being in possession of the ball. Learn how to pass, move and create space. Work hard. Put in the hours. Get good coaching and act upon it. Become accomplished in tiki-taka.

More than ever, what I call stupid footballers won't succeed in the long term as they struggle to compete with the switched-on, smart, strong ones. Over the coming years I predict that an emphasis on the development of football intelligence will become one of the most progressive areas in professional football.

Although Premier League clubs now have vast support staffs in place, to my knowledge there are still only two sports psychologists employed on a full-time basis. To me it's criminal and amazing that most clubs have at least two or three full-time masseurs but no sports psychologist.

In many ways that highlights why this book is so needed in football today. In fact, there has always been a stigma attached to those who seek help with their thinking, and experts in psychology are seen as men in white coats who talk gobbledegook. All complete rubbish of course, yet very few players work on their mental skills. That simply has to change. Football is such big business that it is sheer negligence for owners and their management teams to just leave players to their own devices. It should be seen as a crucial tool to aid peak match-day performance.

During the 2012 Olympics we listened to inspirational Team GB medal winners in cycling, swimming and track-and-field thanking their psychologist for invaluable contributions to their success. Those winners are all constantly looking for what they call 'marginal gains', and they will explore every nook and cranny to find them. Individually these gains might only improve their performance very slightly, but they add up and can eventually make the difference between gold and silver – between winning and losing.

A simple example of a marginal gain: one of the areas that we'll focus on in the book is visualisation, the technique of imagining what you want to achieve. The idea is that you repeatedly picture an event successfully taking place. In football this might be feeling excited and comfortable as you walk out of the tunnel to the pitch, scoring a penalty or a free kick, making a key tackle or crossing the ball. The mental video that is created builds your muscle memory and confidence because your brain can't tell the difference between a real and a vividly imagined experience.

Nowadays visualisation is old news. Most sports and sports performers understand the benefits. Top-class Olympians, Formula One drivers or golfers will tell you that they practise *seeing* themselves participating successfully in their event. Indeed, I'd be surprised if all Team GB's medal winners hadn't used that technique extensively. It's just part of their routine, a healthy habit they've created for themselves. Yet I would guess that only one professional footballer in a thousand does this.

It sounds such an obvious thing to do, yet football remains criminally slow to embrace this kind of thinking. Players need support to improve their on-field performance and support away from match days to cope with the stress and pressure that so many feel. Football is way behind other sports but I'm sure it will learn and improve, and this book is my small contribution to set the ball rolling and encourage it to move in the right direction.

In the chapters that follow I'm going to outline some of the tools and techniques (such as visualisation) that I think will give anyone a psychological edge, in the world of football and beyond.

ROLE MODELS

Each of the subsequent chapters will end with an overview of a role model (or role models) who are particularly proficient in the psychological skills featured in the section. In this one, though, I've focused on examples of players who would be great to follow for those who want to play the tiki-taka way.

Over the last few years the most obvious example of an Englishman who plays the Spanish way has been Paul Scholes. In his younger days Scholes was a goalscoring midfielder, constantly breaking into the box, but as he matured and lost some of his speed he was more inclined to sit in the middle of the pitch where it was his range of passing that really caught the eye.

Paul Scholes: a master conductor of play and perhaps the English footballer most admired by continentals.

He conducted the play for Manchester United, creating space for himself with ease, able to receive and move the ball in the tightest situations, employing a full repertoire of short and long link-play, balls round the corner and probing passes delivered on the run. He hardly ever gave the ball away. Scholes mastered this art steadily, in the company of his talented colleagues, and became the English player most admired by continentals, including the Spanish.

If we turn to the future it's no surprise that we should look to a footballer at Arsenal, where Jack Wilshere has been part of a set-up that has played a fluid, passing game for many years. That's credit to their manager, Arsène Wenger, because he had the foresight of seeing the way football was going and changed the way they played. The Clairefontaine academy near Paris and the total football played by the Dutch international team of the 1970s and 1980s inspired him. The talisman of that team was Johan Cruyff and he transferred those beliefs to the youth structure at Barcelona. Wenger is one who has displayed 2020 vision and persuaded his board at Arsenal to back him.

Arsenal get criticised for the way they play and for overpassing, but they've been very successful for a long time now. They may not win the trophies that some expect, but that may be down to the budget rather than their style of play. Their ethos of how to play is clearly the way the game will evolve.

Of course, Wenger needed footballers with the capabilities and mindset to pass and move like Xavi and Iniesta, and he scoured Europe and beyond to find them – but Wilshere emerged more locally, born in Stevenage and raised in Hitchin. He was only four when Wenger arrived in England from Japan in 1996. Spotted playing for Luton, he practised with Arsenal in 2001 and few have been a more obvious Arsenal and Wenger type of player. So he was fast-tracked to a Premier League debut at 16 years old and a first England cap at 18.

For me he is the standout young midfielder coming through because he appears to have all the qualities that a young Spanish player would have. He's almost like a young Xavi in the way he can pick up the ball and dictate play.

Certainly no other Englishman seems to be able to do what he can do. If you tried to place someone like Jack Rodwell, who is a really good young player, at Barcelona, I think he would struggle because he is more of a stereotypical English player. He's big, strong, has a good engine and good work rate – but if you placed him in the Barcelona or Spanish team I can't imagine that he would fit in very well. He might look out of step, on a different wavelength.

In contrast, if you put Wilshere into the Barcelona or Spanish team I think he would feel and look at home because he is comfortable on the ball, can create space, demand the ball in tight spots, dribble, hold people off, hit both 20-yard and 70-yard passes, and can score goals. He is the ideal candidate for leading the future of English football and has a confidence and sense of belonging that is impressive.

It remains to be seen if injuries stunt his development. But if he gets a clear run in the Premier League and at international level then I would back Wilshere to emerge as the best exponent of tiki-taka in the English game. He will also represent a great role model for young, aspiring professionals to follow – they should watch and learn from him.

KEY MESSAGES

The three main competencies required to be a successful footballer are natural ability, physique and mental skills. In the modern game professionals need to be capable in all these three areas – just having natural ability is nowhere near enough – and they need to excel in at least one. The best of the best are outstanding in all three.

Mental strength is gradually replacing the need for physical strength. Youngsters with a bad attitude and poor mental skills are finding it even more difficult to sustain a career, whereas smart, dedicated footballers are more likely to survive and flourish.

By 2020, football will have further evolved. It will require a quick brain, quick movement and quick feet. The most successful teams will dominate possession and contain switched-on footballers. The game will become more technical but with less physical contact. By then the game will, at long last, have followed other sports in finding ways to develop the mental strength of its participants. Working with specialists in this area will no longer be seen as a weakness but simply as a way of achieving peak performance.

LESSON ONE

TAKE PERSONAL RESPONSIBILITY

Stupid footballers moan, blame others and play the victim – and for world-class whinging then pre-season training is the place to be. It is undoubtedly demanding, the hardest time for a professional footballer. For six to seven weeks you have three sessions a day, burning up to 6000 calories. Your body is put through stresses that you don't go through during the season. However, it is absolutely critical to give you a strong foundation of fitness and prepare you for the season ahead.

Yet many players moan from beginning to end, trying to get away with doing the minimum. This is crazy because when the season starts they are the ones who will enjoy the benefit. They'll have the preparation, the strength in their legs, the ability to run. So their attitude is misplaced and misguided. They should actually be thanking the coaches and manager for putting them through it and for their motivation and encouragement.

Of course the attitude to pre-season training continues when the games start. Mental and emotional habits have been formed. Through the season they still think that they are being controlled, whether it's the manager telling them when to come in for training, the fitness coach making them run or the nutritionist instructing them what to eat. So they have the resistance of followers – and this negative, victim mentality seeps into the dressing room and on to the pitch during matches.

For example, in my experience some always thought it was the manager's fault that they weren't playing in the team, when actually that is never the case unless he is making a tactical decision to rotate his squad and rest players. Generally the manager wants to play the players who are training the best and performing on match days, if only to help him keep his job. He never wants to put out a weakened team that is more likely to lose.

Surprise surprise, it was mainly the ones who moaned and complained who didn't get selected, drifted out of the team and the squad, got released and started to slide down the leagues. Of course, all the way down they were blaming others rather than looking at themselves. They may have achieved a certain amount in their football career through a natural ability, physique, technical ability and tactical awareness. But they couldn't sustain it or consistently achieve peak performance because they weren't able to use a range of psychological tools to prepare. They weren't football smart.

During my career I played with several who loved a moan. I think part of this is cultural. In society as a whole many just like to complain, forgetting about all the good. It's also part of the culture in football, where young, enthusiastic apprentices can gradually get sucked into that mindset; not least, I think, because many inside the game don't always realise how lucky they are. For many it's all they've ever known.

Certainly in football there are loads of opportunities to blame easy targets and play the victim if you want to. You can moan about the training, the manager, your teammates, the pitch, the fans, the referee, the media and the pressure. But it's only the stupid ones that keep doing that, because it definitely has a negative impact on them psychologically, and that affects how well they play.

Just to emphasise, I'm not highlighting the moaners for the sake of it. I'm doing it because it is so important. What seems like harmless whinging is nothing of the sort. It usually leads to blaming others and to playing the victim – all unhealthy traits that create a culture of negativity within the team.

The English football squad that went to the 2010 World Cup in South Africa epitomised this. When I saw that they were widely reported as being bored in their base at Phokeng near Rustenburg I was completely flabbergasted. They'd just spent two years qualifying for the greatest tournament in world football. For many it was the pinnacle of their careers, and it presented a golden opportunity to showcase their talents and shine on the biggest possible stage in front of a global audience of billions. Yet they were bored.

Germany weren't bored. Prior to the meeting of the two nations in the round of 16 all their energies were focused on beating England, getting to the quarter-finals, semi-finals and then to the final – which is what they always want to do in tournaments. That's the German mentality.

Germany didn't win that match 4–1 because they had more talent. It was because they had a completely different state of mind within the squad and took that into the game. They must have laughed at the poor, bored Englishmen. One team took a winners' mentality on to the pitch, the other one didn't.

Certainly I found that taking personal responsibility for the choices I made needed to become a part of my psychological toolkit. I've never been a big moaner. Even as a child I was cheerful, and during my career when I had grievances and frustrations I kept them out of the dressing room. But I needed a couple of harsh lessons before the penny began to drop for me in making my own choices and taking responsibility for myself.

The first came when I was in my first year in Tottenham's youth team, living in Enfield with some of the other players. At that stage I was innocent and easily led astray. Most days after training we went to a local pub, played on the fruit machines and enjoyed a pub lunch that was a long way from an athlete's diet – as well as a few drinks. We'd do that three or four times a week as well as going out some evenings. It wasn't something I thought about or analysed. I certainly didn't consider that we were being unprofessional. That was just the way it was.

Then one Friday night I was encouraged by some young pros to come out for a few drinks. They didn't have a game the next day, but I did. One drink led to another and I staggered home, completely drunk at 2 a.m., precisely six and a half hours before I was picked up by the team bus to travel to our youth team game against Brentford. By that stage the hangover hadn't even kicked in. When we reached the ground I got changed into my kit and went on to the training pitch to warm up with the team. For some reason the manager was not around, and while the other lads did their stretches I lay on my back on the pitch, put my hands behind my head, shut my eyes and enjoyed the rays of warm spring sunshine on my face. I was still drunk, enjoying the buzz of a good night out.

What was remarkable was my performance when the game started. For 45 minutes I was Lionel Messi and Cristiano Ronaldo rolled into one. I had never played better before and I never played better afterwards. Everything I attempted came off. I torpedoed 50-yard diagonals like an American football quarterback; I set my partner up front, Rory Allen, away with a defence-splitting pass to open the scoring; then I scored myself with a left-foot half volley into the top corner that would have graced Wembley Stadium. But, as commentators often say, half time came at the wrong time. Back in the changing room I hit the wall, and a pounding head, chronic dehydration and a complete absence of energy replaced my alcoholic buzz. Although I started the second half I was a complete shambles. I couldn't run, kept giving the ball away, had no coordination – and after 10 minutes the manager put me out of my misery. For the rest of that day I was a mess, totally wrecked. In some ways I got away with it as for some reason the manager never questioned me about my hero-to-zero performance, but when I sobered up I did think 'what the hell am I doing?'

Certainly it was the stupidest thing I'd ever done, and while I began by blaming the lads who led me astray I eventually realised that I needed to take responsibility for my own actions or risk wasting the opportunity that I had worked so hard for.

My second and harshest lesson came in the summer of 1997. This was during my time at Tottenham Hotspur. I made my debut for them against Aston Villa, played a couple of games at the end of the 1996/1997 season, and scored in my home debut against Coventry. I thought I had cracked it and went home to Belfast for the summer thinking I was pretty much a fully fledged Premier League player.

A goal for Tottenham on my home debut against Coventry. The celebrations went on all summer!

So I had a great summer. I was out all the time enjoying myself, drinking, socialising and going on holidays. I came back for the start of pre-season unfit, overweight and out of shape. No matter; I thought pre-season was about running off the excesses of the summer and getting fit for the start of the season. But the sports scientist at the club ran a series of tests that highlighted that my fitness levels were way, way below the others. In truth I was never really able to catch them up. It affected my ability to play at my best during the 1997/1998 season, and when the club ultimately released me that complacency during the previous summer was a contributory factor. That time, I was the stupid footballer.

Fortunately, that pre-season gave me the kick up the backside I needed. I realised that it is okay to relax, go on holiday and have fun in the six-week break between seasons, but that I also needed to prepare my body to be ready for another 11-month stint. So I never made the same mistake again, and I looked after myself. There were some phases in my career when I chose to follow disciplined, elite professional athletes such as Arsenal and Holland's superstar Dennis Bergkamp, who I believe only drank water throughout his whole footballing career. I can see how that would that have helped him greatly, and for two years in the middle of my career I was also teetotal and regimented in my preparation for, and recovery from, games.

Yet I ultimately made the choice that to keep a balance between my personal life and my career I was content to risk being 5–10 per cent less successful on the pitch if the payback was happy, enjoyable times with friends, family and teammates off the pitch.

That was partly due to the fact that of all the potential distractions that tease athletes, I think I struggled most to turn my back on opportunities to socialise and have a few drinks. I didn't feel stress and pressure in the way that many do from playing the actual games, but I found the personal discipline that is required to live the lifestyle of the ultimate professional a challenge. There were times that I felt I needed to let my hair down as a release from the intensity of preparation and recovery.

It probably didn't help that during my career (although times have moved on) there was a drinking culture in professional football. By that I mean that many of the players often went out together on Saturdays – and Tuesdays if there was no midweek game – to drink. While it might not have been ideal for physical conditioning it did help the team to gel and bond. Some of the fondest memories I have of the Norwich City squad that got promoted to the Premiership in 2003/2004 are the nights we had out together.

I'd emphasise that this 'work hard–play hard' approach was a conscious choice that I made in how I wanted to live my life and I took full responsibility for the implications. Equally, don't confuse the socialising with any lack of commitment or laziness. I kept working hard, perhaps harder, on the training ground so that my performances on the pitch didn't suffer.

So although I enjoyed some great holidays in fun-filled locations such as Las Vegas during the off-season and seized the opportunity to unwind, I also trained every day, still did weights three times a week and worked as hard as during the season because I wanted to return for pre-season as fit as when I left – if not fitter. And I was certainly a better footballer for it, not just because I was fitter but also because I got into the habit of taking responsibility for myself and brought that mindset to training and match days.

I think Stephen Carr, who played for Spurs for 10 years, then Newcastle and Birmingham, went through a similar experience. As a young professional he enjoyed the social side and a few drinks, but then the club doctor told him that he wasn't going to have a long-term career if he didn't stop drinking, and he suddenly took responsibility and chose to turn himself into a model pro, someone who I looked up to. His professionalism was incredible because everything he did was about trying to improve himself.

Often the likes of Stephen Carr have a positive impact on the players around them. Roy Keane set high standards and was such a winner that he insisted upon focus and commitment from others on the pitch and could be hard on those who didn't meet his expectations. But don't confuse that with the moaning I mentioned earlier in the chapter. Keane's demands came from a good place. He wanted his teammates to play better and the team to win. That's very different from whinging because you've been asked to do something.

Smart footballers recognise that they train for only a couple of hours a day and get paid very, very well for it. They know it is a dream job – kicking a ball around with your mates, something that you used to do for nothing. And when I had the mindset of appreciating the abundance of incredibly good things in my life, then I went into games of football (and every other activity) more positively, loving the whole experience, giving and getting more out of myself.

I think it came down to recognising that, whatever I was doing, *I* had chosen to be in that position. No one else. Most people seem to think that someone else is making the choices for them, writing their life script, when actually no one ever has their arm up your back.

There are footballers that go into training with a bad attitude, thinking 'oh God, I have got to go to train'. But actually they don't have to if they don't want to. They can quit and travel the world if they like. It's their choice. They just have to accept the consequences – and that is true for all of us in all walks of life.

So we always have a choice in everything that we do, but people who don't realise that and don't fully accept and understand the principle will be prone to moan, to blame someone else. It will always be external forces and factors that they blame, rather than accepting that it's down to them.

Understanding this was certainly one of my biggest breakthroughs as a footballer and as a person. After my experience at Tottenham I tried to get as much out of training sessions as I could. So I practised new skills that I hadn't tried before and always gave 100 per cent. I wanted the manager to see me as reliable, know that I was giving it my all in every session and that when I went into matches I would be totally prepared to play at my best. With that mindset why would I ever moan about being there?

I also chose to change my attitude after games. In the first few years of playing I blamed myself if the team lost or I didn't play well. I would beat myself up over the weekend through to Monday and sometimes into Tuesday or Wednesday. That wasn't helpful, and once I realised I could consciously change my mindset I took a step back, looked at the big picture and asked 'is beating myself up actually going to help me with my football?' The answer was 'no, not at all'. So I changed my approach.

Since then – now that I have moved out of professional football – I do everything with a positive demeanour because I think 'if not, why would I do it?' If I don't want to do something then I don't. This is the opposite of most people, who wake up on a Monday morning and feel like they have to go to work, when they don't really want to.

It is certainly critical for a younger player to understand their motives for wanting to be a professional footballer. So many get caught up in the material things, the lifestyle and the trappings – wanting to be on TV, drive fast cars – but actually they are all secondary to the reasons why people actually make it as a professional footballer. I don't know any professional footballer who was initially driven by money, although I do accept that as they get older and have families, mortgages and other responsibilities that may change.

But youngsters need to really enjoy playing the game because the majority won't play in the Premier League and so won't earn big money or be famous. When they go to play Carlisle on a Tuesday night in January then will they really want to travel on a bus for seven hours to go and play the game, then travel back for seven hours, get up and go to training the next day?

The answer needs to be yes.

Because if they are not going for the actual joy of playing football and accepting everything that goes with it then it is going to be difficult for them to perform at their best. Ultimately, unless they have that real passion and enthusiasm for football then their career will probably be short-lived and they'll become another Rory Allen. I was at Tottenham Hotspur in the youth set-up with Rory. He was undoubtedly talented, but he always said that he hated football, even after he had earned a long-term professional contract, got into the first team and scored against Manchester United – most people's idea of a dream come true. After his time at Spurs Harry Redknapp took him to Portsmouth for £1 million on about £6000 a week.

So you'd think Rory was doing pretty well and would be happy and content. But one day he didn't turn up for training. They tried his mobile, but no answer. Next day was the same, and the next. By now people were getting worried. Everyone was saying 'has anyone seen Rory Allen?', but no one knew where he was until a national newspaper published a picture of him with the Barmy Army cricket fans in Australia watching the Ashes. He never came back to play professional football. So because he didn't have a genuine passion to play the game he ultimately gave up a lucrative career.

I give him credit for making that choice, if that's how he felt. Most would have plodded along, taken the weekly salary, felt like a victim and that others were in charge of their life – and their performances, personal happiness and sense of fulfilment would surely have continued to deteriorate. At least he made a clear and positive choice, although it might have been an idea for him to tell someone.

So – with Rory in mind – when I mentor young footballers who tell me they want to play at the highest level I question them: do you really want to play football for a living? How much? Why? Do you appreciate that you must take responsibility for every choice and decision you make?

If the answers to those questions are positive then all things are possible. If the answers are negative then my advice to them is to stop now, stop wasting their time and the people who are supporting them, find something that they have a genuine passion for and put their energy into that instead.

ROLE MODEL

Taking personal responsibility is never more important than in adversity, and anyone who plays sport knows that there will be times when they are up against it. In fact one of the attractions and frustrations of sport lies is its unpredictability. Every performer enjoys highs and suffers lows. They win and they lose; their personal fortunes ebb and flow, as do the teams that they play for. That's just the way it is.

But what happened to Fernando Torres, the centre-forward from Spain, was not the norm, not something that could easily be explained by the law of averages. Rarely have I seen an elite performer reach the peak of his profession and then perform as badly as he did through much of 2011 and into 2012. The media and many fans crucified him. To some he became a figure of fun. So the fact that he overcame that long slump by returning to form with Champions League and European Championship medals makes him a fascinating example to analyse.

Fernando Torres: at his peak he was possibly the best striker on the planet. Since then his mental strength has been challenged by dips in form.

For most of his career Torres had only known success. He started in his native Spain with Atletico Madrid and became known as 'El Niño' ('the kid') for his prolific goal scoring. In 2007 he deservedly attracted the interest of Liverpool, who paid out a record transfer fee, and the goals just kept coming. He became the fastest player in Liverpool history to score 50 league goals, and at that time I would have rated him as the best centre-forward in the world. He could do everything – he made great runs into space, he was quick, could pick it up deep and above all he could score – with tap-ins, headers, volleys, long-range efforts. In fact he was a threat from pretty much anywhere and helped Liverpool to challenge for the title, combining brilliantly with Steven Gerrard.

He also starred on the international stage for Spain. He scored three times at the 2006 World Cup, twice at the 2008 Euros – including the winner over Germany in the final – and became a World Cup winner in 2010. Torres seemed to have the world at his feet, yet for both Spain and Liverpool he gradually went off the boil, not helped by a series of niggling injuries. The goals had begun to dry up even before Chelsea paid a record British transfer fee of £50 million for him – and at first it looked like they had made a hugely expensive mistake.

During the 2011/2012 Premier League season Torres failed to score between 24 September, 2011 and 31 March, 2012. In total his dry period stretched for over a year and it was nowhere near the return that Chelsea were looking for on such a massive investment. I'm not sure that any other centre-forward at a Premier League club would have been persevered with for so long. Anyone else would have been dropped or sold. He couldn't score for love nor money; going from 20 or 30 goals every season to nothing. From being arguably the best striker on the planet he became one of the worst in the Premier League.

Of course, when you are a sporting icon your performances always come under the microscope. Every missed chance was endlessly analysed and dissected. He had nowhere to hide from this public embarrassment. So why did El Niño turn into a no-hoper?

During that nightmare period he had lost none of his genetic gifts of ball sense and coordination. Nor had he lost his skills, technique or physical capability. Maybe injuries had taken the edge off his blistering pace, but that would have been balanced out by his increasing experience and tactical awareness. So the only explanation for his slump in performance lay in the grey matter between his ears. His manager at Chelsea, Roberto Di Matteo, admitted as much when he said that Torres 'had a psychological block'.

I don't know Torres and I don't know what that psychological block was. But I have no doubt that he lost confidence and started to think too much rather than just play instinctively and trust his ability. It looked like he had no self-belief and no enthusiasm for playing. As the run went on he needed to think more constructively to turn things around. He had to be strong, to keep a positive self-image, to focus on what he wanted to achieve, not what he wanted to avoid, and above all, he needed to take responsibility for his performances, to acknowledge there was a problem and that he would do everything he could to try to improve the situation.

It would have been easy for Torres to blame external factors: the transfer fee, the injuries, the move of clubs, the tactics and system played at Chelsea, his teammates, the manager, bad luck. Many would have done so and that would have made things worse. It would have led to an even deeper downward spiral. But, to his credit, Torres didn't do that. He admitted that his performances were down to him and that only he could put them right. There is a saying that 'if you don't like your reflection don't blame the mirror', and he certainly didn't blame the mirror. He knew it was his responsibility to score goals and he knew he wasn't doing it. It takes a lot to say 'I'm not good enough at the minute' and to share that with the world, but I think he knew, deep down, that his ability was still there and that his fortunes would turn around at some stage if he kept persevering. In fact he said 'I'm 27, I don't forget how to score goals. I will score again.'

For me performances are always down to the player. There's no point blaming others. That's just futile. But quotes from people in the know provide confirmation that even when things looked bleak Torres kept working hard, was mentally resilient and took responsibility for turning it around.

His ex-manager at Liverpool, Roy Hodgson, said that Torres was an 'outstanding player' and a 'very good person'. He explained that all strikers go through barren patches and they have to be strong to deal with it. But he backed Torres, adding 'he's working very hard. I'd certainly back him to succeed because he's a very good professional. I've got nothing but good to say about him.'

And ex-Chelsea striker Andrei Shevchenko said: 'When a club has paid a lot of money for you, that obviously brings its own pressures but you just have to go out and do your best on the pitch and I know Torres does that. Great strikers don't suddenly forget how to score goals . . . The goals will come for him.'

And, of course, eventually they did. After he got his first goal for months, a half-hit shot on a rainy pitch, he began to get his positivity back again. He began running at defenders, he looked driven and focused – and the goals followed. It culminated in the semi-final of the Champions League at Barcelona when Torres came on as a substitute. In the last minute, with the game on a knife-edge and Chelsea hanging on against wave after wave of Barca attacks, Chelsea had a counterattack. Torres made a great run, was played through one-on-one against goalkeeper Víctor Valdés and went round him with consummate ease to score and take his team into the final. That was when I thought 'he's back'.

Five days later he scored the first hat-trick of his Chelsea career. He also helped them to beat Bayern Munich to win the 2012 Champions League and scored three goals in the 2012 Euros to win the Golden Boot, as part of the trailblazing Spanish international team.

Is Torres back to his previous best? I'm not sure he's quite at the pinnacle anymore but he's 97–98 per cent there, and I would expect his career to have fewer peaks and troughs from now on. All forwards suffer from periods where the goals dry up, but I doubt it will be so extreme in the future. Certainly I know that Torres only dug himself out of that hole by taking responsibility – and for that he has my admiration.

KEY MESSAGES

It is imperative that we make the choice to take responsibility for our own actions, particularly in adversity. It can provide a real breakthrough in how we think and behave.

It is difficult to take personal responsibility and be successful if we fundamentally undertake activities 'against our will'. It is better to be clear about what we want to achieve, take responsibility for making it happen and then have a positive and upbeat demeanour. That is much more likely to lead to better results and outcomes.

There are lots of moaners in all walks of life, and the danger is that this leads to a negative mentality, blaming others and playing the victim.

CREATE A HELPFUL SELF-IMAGE

If you were asked to describe yourself in detail to a stranger what would you say? What kind of person are you? What are your strengths and weaknesses? What stage of your development are you at? What will you be achieving in the future?

Your current self-image will determine how you answered those questions. It reflects your beliefs and has been created by an ever-changing mental picture of yourself made up of your own perception of what you look like; your personality; the status you think you have achieved in your personal or professional life; your skills, attributes and capabilities; and what you think you are capable of.

Self-image can be influenced by the views of others and events as they unfold – but ultimately it is self-created. Your mental picture might not match what many others think; yet it will be influential throughout your life. Certainly my self-image was highly influential in my sporting career – as can be seen by detailing how it rose and fell during the early stages.

As I entered big-time football I allowed my self-image to be largely created by the opinions of others. Because I had been the best player in pretty much all of my teams as I was growing up, and had been contracted by Tottenham Hotspur, I received plenty of praise. Each pat on the back bolstered my confidence and pampered my ego. Understandably I felt I was a promising young footballer, a bit special, so I was full of confidence, a big fish that had only swum in small ponds.

But that self-image deflated in my first few minutes as a bona fide professional footballer in July 1994 as I walked out in my new training kit for my first day of pre-season training as a professional footballer at Tottenham Hotspur and spotted World Cup superstar Jürgen Klinsmann in the distance. Within an awestruck second I was back to being a shy 16-year-old, newly off the plane from Belfast, a long way from home and a lot further away from ever emulating the achievements of such a footballing icon.

In the 1990s Klinsmann was one of the biggest names in football, right up there with the likes of Diego Maradona. He was one of the German World Cup-winning team in 1990; he made 108 international appearances and scored 47 goals, including scoring in three consecutive World Cups (11 goals in total) and three consecutive European Championships. He played club football for Stuttgart, Inter Milan, Bayern Munich and Sampdoria.

So you can imagine my reaction when I found that I would be working on the same training ground as Klinsmann on my first day. It was also his first day at the club. He'd just been signed from AS Monaco in France for £2 million.

I was totally in awe of Klinsmann, as were all of the youth team wannabes. We had been watching him on TV at the World Cup just three weeks earlier and were thinking 'what a legend, what a superstar'. I remained in awe of him throughout much of that season. Klinsmann was playing at a level and had self-assurance, an aura, which I felt I couldn't hope to replicate. He scored on his debut and became a fans' favourite, scoring 21 goals that season.

Nor was it just Klinsmann who had an aura. When I was a first year pro at Tottenham Teddy Sheringham had just finished being part of the England squad at the 1996 European Championships. It was a tournament where England caught football fever. Everyone was singing 'it's coming home' and Teddy was one of the leading lights within the team, scoring twice against Holland in the 4–1 victory and then slotting away his penalty in the semi-final shoot out against Germany when England went out of the tournament.

So when he came back to Tottenham for pre-season he had acquired megastar status. He was known internationally, the best player on our team and on the most money – but what struck me was that he was so modest and down to earth. He'd come and sit down and chat with me in the canteen. That made me feel amazing and want to model myself on him.

In addition to his humility I also loved the way he played the game. He was just so smart, by far the cleverest I've played with and far ahead of everybody in his thinking. He would always pull opposition defenders into positions they didn't want to be in. He would step up a yard and the defender would come with him. He'd step another yard and the defender would come with him. He'd step another yard and the defender now knew he was three yards away from the rest of his defence so would need to let him go or go with him and leave a massive gap behind. Nine times out of ten they would drop back in, and Sheringham was suddenly in space in that hole between the midfield and the defence.

That cleverness was why he developed this priceless gift of being able to create five yards of space for himself – not just in the hole but also in a crowded penalty box full of defenders. And when the chance came to him his finishing was outstanding. I think he had a natural aptitude, but every day he would do extra finishing practice because he knew what ultimately paid his wages.

So I was learning an awful lot from Teddy, while never imagining that I could emulate him. He had a self-assurance and conviction that I couldn't even imagine.

For the whole two years I was in the youth team I was coming into contact with players like Klinsmann and Sheringham. Darren Anderton, Nicky Barmby, Sol Campbell and David Ginola were also top-class performers and I just couldn't imagine playing in the same team. When I saw them at training I just thought 'how am I ever going to get to their level?' I didn't believe I could. I was just a kid from Belfast.

I guess it was understandable that I was in awe of these legends at that stage. I was simply content that I had similar ability to the others in the youth team. However, at that stage my perception of my capabilities and potential was not conducive to me achieving my ambitions in the game: becoming a first-team player and playing international football.

Even when I was a paid professional training with the first-teamers every day, and supposedly competing with them for a place in the team, my confidence didn't grow. I just didn't see myself as a first-teamer. I never thought I could do it.

So praise be to Rory Allen – the same Rory Allen who ultimately decided that playing a game he hated was not a good way to spend his waking life and gave up the sport. Rory had come through the youth team with me. He had no more ability but got an opportunity through an injury to Chris Armstrong, the regular first-team striker.

Rory took his chance in style, scoring goals including one against Manchester United. He didn't know what he had done. Not only had he made a name for himself but he had upgraded what his mates in the reserves thought they were capable of. Up until then we didn't think we were good enough for the first team. Some of us probably thought we might get there some day, others not. However, if Rory could do it then so could we. Not only did he break into the team physically, but psychologically he had broken down the biggest barrier.

Rory's flying start opened the floodgates. Our beliefs changed in an instant. Others made it into the first team, including myself three months later. That was a real key moment. I realised that because I'd never *seen* myself as a first-team player my self-image had been stopping me. I realised that it was something that I could help to create rather than something that just happens. Above all I realised how powerful it would be in helping me to achieve my ambitions in football.

Certainly by the time I made my debut I had been scoring goals in the reserves and felt I was worthy of my chance. That confidence and self-belief were critical in allowing me to play well in three games at the end of that season. So it was a psychological improvement in what I thought I was capable of that led to the physical achievement.

This often happens. For years people believed it was impossible for a man to run a mile in under four minutes. Doctors and scientists said that the human body could not possibly achieve such a feat; some suggested that the body would break apart before such a speed could be reached.

But after breaking the 1500 metres record, an athlete called Dr Roger Bannister made a psychological breakthrough. He could see himself breaking the barrier, a belief that made all the difference. Again the psychological breakthrough led to the physical achievement – and in May 1954 he ran a mile in 3 minutes 59.4 seconds. Once he had proven that it could be done, others had tangible evidence. Although it was an illusion, Bannister's run gave them belief – he almost gave them permission.

What happened next was almost as extraordinary as Bannister's achievement: 46 days later the record was broken again; in the next 30 years the record was broken 16 more times; in 50 years no less than 17 seconds were sliced off the record; and since Bannister thousands have run the mile in under four minutes. It just needed someone to show it was possible and lead the way. Once the belief was there, the rest was inevitable, as long as it was backed by desire.

The stories about Rory and Roger highlight two key learning points. First, that I was placing unhelpful limitations upon myself. It is a social condition, particularly within our culture: people are all too quick to say 'don't get too big for your boots', 'don't be a big head', 'don't be up yourself'. It's seen as good to be modest. The danger is that the words we use – both to others and to ourselves – reinforce this modesty until we believe it and it becomes our self-image.

Research suggests that on average we have images and an inner voice communicating to us about 70 per cent of the time. This self-talk is bound to have an impact because we naturally learn through repetition. So I came to learn that whatever I tell myself continually reinforces that belief and has an impact on the way I view myself.

Often my self-talk was modest:

- I'm never going to break into the first team.
- I'm never going to be a professional footballer.
- They're in a different league.
- I'll never be as good as him.
- I'm not as good as I was before the injury.
- We're never going to win the league.
- We're going down.

But over time I trained myself to use more positive beliefs:

- I can do that too.
- I'm as good as he is.
- I'm improving.
- I'm feeling more confident.
- Today, I feel strong.
- I can play professional football.
- I'm going to score today.
- We're going to win.

Either way, this self-talk signposted my mental state and beliefs and had consequences in my actions and behaviour because more of the kinds of things I thought and talked about became a reality. So there became no place for false modesty in my thinking. I'm not advocating arrogance, but having a high opinion of yourself is the only way to push yourself to achieve what you are capable of.

The second point here is that while Rory and Roger were the catalysts, the barrier-breakers, they didn't give the others belief and confidence. That would have been impossible. Belief can't actually be given to you. It is an internal feeling that only you can create. In those early years at Tottenham I was limiting myself, and because of that I was the only one who could change it. Ultimately it was me who broke the threshold in my head.

So my fluctuating self image had sky-rocketed to an all-time high, with my inner voice bursting with confidence once I got into the first team and did well. I felt like I was a fully fledged first team and Premier League player on the tenuous basis of three games and one goal. In fact I went into the kind of celebration mode that more appropriately accompanies winning the World Cup. Unfortunately, I thought that I had finished my hard work, whereas I should have realised that it would be harder to stay in the first team and keep improving.

Certainly the next few years put paid to any illusions of grandeur. A three-year contract followed my one-year contract, but through my lack of fitness, injuries and limited opportunities I allowed my self-image to drop. I lost the belief that I could make it at Spurs, and that was a view that was entirely shared by the then manager, George Graham. Even if I didn't quite see myself as an established first-team player at Tottenham I didn't stop believing that I could play football professionally.

When I went to Norwich the challenge felt different. Although I needed to prove myself at a different club I knew that I was capable of doing well.

Goal! A last-gasp winner for Norwich City against Reading. One of the best feelings in the world – sometimes it's pure ecstasy.

There were no superstars at Norwich; instead I was competing for a place alongside players who were on a par with me. I spent a year in the reserves, scoring goals, getting fitter and stronger, training hard, developing my technique, until, at the age of 22, I knew I was ready for Norwich's first team.

I just needed the opportunity, and it came under manager Nigel Worthington when an injury to Chris Llewellyn gave me my chance against Manchester City on the left wing. I scored, we won 2–0 and I cemented my place, becoming a regular in the side and eventually racking up 288 appearances for Norwich over six years.

By then I had developed good habits in bolstering my self-image because I had become aware of my use of language and the significance of it. I used techniques that were relevant outside of football and, since leaving the professional game, I am still using them to good effect.

For instance, I use what are known as 'formal affirmations' to build my confidence. I write down a phrase with a desired trait, then recite it like a mantra each day. When I left football I was petrified of speaking in public, but because I wanted to work in the media, each day for 18 months I recited the phrase 'I love speaking in public'. At the start I was saying it but it wasn't a reality and felt awkward. However, I kept saying it and eventually it became a reality. The more I practise and the more I use affirmations, the better I get. Now I really do love speaking in public, and that's no coincidence.

So how has this analysis of the ebb and flow of my self-image highlighted areas where I developed my thinking?

ONE

I learned to be aware of the importance of how I viewed myself. I listened to both the language that I used to others and my inner voice. Everything I say has a consequence.

TWO

Self-image is not something that has to go up and down depending on what happens and what others say about you. Only those with a weaker mentality allow that. When they perform well and others praise them then their self-image rises; if they perform badly and receive criticism then it falls. But that's not helpful.

THREE

I became aware that most of us have a self-image that limits our potential and does not allow us to achieve what we are able to achieve. Because it's a reality that we have created and only exists in our heads, it can be changed in an instant.

For those three reasons this is an area that I now consciously work hard on developing. I work constructively on my self-talk and affirmations to build up my self-image. I try to programme myself to change my habits and use language that tells myself and others what I can do, what I want to do and what I am capable of.

The benefits of making these changes have been an improved performance, a more robust self-confidence, and a greater ability to cope with pressure and setbacks.

ROLE MODELS

The world's greatest footballer, Lionel Messi, could appear as a role model in any one of the chapters. He has a great attitude towards football, and in addition to his mental approach he has immense natural, tactical and technical ability, and the speed to ease away from opponents as though they don't exist. Being five foot six inches in height is no hindrance to him.

Lionel Messi: phenomenal skills and a great attitude – both confident and humble.

However, what strikes me most about Messi is the way that his self-image helps him both on and off the pitch. On the pitch there is swagger and arrogance in his play because he knows when he gets the ball he can do whatever he wants with it. He is totally confident in his capabilities, knowing that is he is able to outwit the best domestic, European and international defences. Clearly he has placed no psychological barriers on what he is capable of achieving – otherwise how could he be able to boast this impressive list of achievements:

- The only player to win to win four Ballons d'Or
- Five La Liga titles
- Three Champions League titles

- Top scorer in four successive Champions League campaigns
- Most goals (91) scored in a calendar year (2012), beating Gerd Müller's record, including 79 for Barcelona

You could argue that these amazing feats are comparable to Sir Roger Bannister's four-minute mile because they can only be achieved by someone whose self-image allows them to break records. Yet Messi's swagger and arrogance are left on the pitch. Once he returns to civilisation he becomes a humble, modest, normal lad from Argentina again.

Don't underestimate how difficult it is not to get carried away. It would be so easy for him to do a George Best and waste his talent, throwing his career away because he wanted to spend his time in nightclubs and his money on fast cars. His ego could swell and he could see himself as superhuman, above the law.

Several in the English game have struggled to cope with fame. Paul Gascoigne is one; Tony Adams also comes to mind. And, as I've explained elsewhere in this book, I started partying like I'd just won the World Cup after a couple of end-of-season games for Tottenham. Messi could be forgiven if he boasted about his ability and, like Muhammad Ali, told anyone who wanted to listen that he was 'the greatest!' In truth not many people could argue with him if he did.

Yet if his self-image was of a superstar celebrity then he could easily get caught up in all the hype, adulation and circus that surrounds the best players in football – and I'm certain that it would eventually detract from what first got him into that position. Fortunately that's just not in his nature. For Messi it's all about the game. He is obsessed with football to the exclusion of everything else. The fame, the money, the endorsements, the celebrity lifestyle – if it interests him at all then it is secondary to the simple pleasure of playing.

Before one Champions League Final Messi said 'I will just go on the pitch and do as I always do, play every game as if it were my last'. That just about sums him up. He's a shy, ordinary guy living an extraordinary life. His teammate at Barcelona, Gerard Piqué, said: 'Being the best player in history, he could behave in a different way but he is just such a lovely person, creating a great atmosphere in the dressing-room'; and Chemi Terés, the club's press chief, added: 'I've known him a long time and he has never changed at all. Quiet, doesn't want to show off. His character and attitude is exemplary. He's a very simple man, a family man, who loves more than anything else to play football.'

What makes Messi's mentality outstanding to me is the fact that he has created a self-image that allows him the confidence to achieve great feats on the pitch, but the humility to manage his lifestyle away from football in a way that allows him to prepare and rest in the right way. That is a trick that is almost impossible to achieve – and he has my undying admiration, not just for his skill but the way he conducts himself.

Before I leave the subject of Messi and his self-image I just want to raise something that might be controversial.

Messi has the benefit of having a positive and constructive self-image that is reinforced by all the adulation he receives. I don't think that is true of two long-standing English internationals, John Terry and Ashley Cole. In comparison they are unpopular, even in their own country. Terry, in particular, has been surrounded by a series of controversies and incidents, and has been on the front pages of newspapers as much as the back. Other than Chelsea fans few seem to have a good word to say about them, yet they have clearly retained a self-image that has allowed them to have illustrious careers with the kinds of achievements that deserve to see them ranked as two of England's greatest modern-day players.

Whilst I'm not passing judgement on some of the controversies, I do applaud the fact that they have not allowed the negative feedback and unpopularity to affect their self-image and their performances on the pitch. They have both been consistently high-quality performers who always deliver. Love them or hate them, you'd want to have them in your team.

KEY MESSAGES

Most of us don't have a self-image that allows us to achieve what we want. We place unhelpful limitations upon ourselves, reinforced by an unduly modest self-talk (inner voice), which signposts our mental state and beliefs.

Self-image is largely defined by our personal beliefs and is a positive asset when it is in alignment with what we want to achieve. We can only achieve what our self-image allows us to, so psychological breakthroughs often lead to the actual achievement.

While self-image is often influenced by the views of others and by events, they can only have this influence if we allow them to. In fact, our self-image can only be created by ourselves, and we can do so by repeating affirmations.

LESSON THREE

DEFINE AND FOLLOW GOALS

Goals have always played a large part in both my sporting and personal life. As a striker, scoring goals was the ultimate in happiness, a moment of indescribable elation that I was lucky enough to enjoy 43 times in my professional career. But off the pitch goals have become equally significant for me, helping me to improve my performance and achieve my ambitions.

During my childhood in Belfast there were always bombs going off, tanks driving down my street and soldiers walking past my house with rifles on their arms. Football was my outlet, and I developed a love and a natural aptitude for the game. I daydreamed of playing professionally across the water in England, and my parents remember me telling them about my aspirations when I was in the bath aged just seven. At that stage, though, it was no more than a vague, misty ambition that I didn't really believe would come true. It was through raw talent and luck rather than design that things kept working out and I found myself at the illustrious Tottenham Hotspur Football Club. It was only as I matured that I adopted a more structured approach to help me perform at my best.

The mists began to clear for me when I was 17 years old and one of my mentors, Tim Ball, gave me a book called *Awaken the Giant Within* written by the American guru and author, Tony Robbins. To say it struck a chord would be an understatement. It was a brilliant wake-up call, and every word made perfect sense to me. He wrote about projecting. Where did I see myself in three years' time? Or five years' time? He wrote about how everyone has all the resources they need to be successful within themselves. Yet many people focus on external factors and place an excessive emphasis on their importance. Most significantly, he explained that success doesn't happen by accident. It doesn't come to you. You have to seek it out and make it happen.

Absorbed, I read it all, more than once, took copious notes, made lists and created action plans. I still remember the little inscription in the book from my mentor: 'To your success. November 1995'. Suitably inspired, I sat down and for the first time began planning my goals in detail. In fact I still have them, on some sheets of A4 paper that are now browning with age.

Using a structure suggested in the book I focused on the main areas in my life. The one relating to football contains the goal to stop eating junk food.

I had written the overall title of 'forces that shape your life' and then came up with the following, which related to the goal:

- Actions I have been putting off? Stop eating fast foods.
- Why haven't I taken action? I think I enjoy eating these foods and the convenience.
- Pleasure from indulging in the negative pattern? I think they are tasty and easily accessible.
- What will it cost me if I don't change now? I could lose my place in the team and lose £1 million in career money.

Ever since then I have set goals that have given me purpose and helped me to plan how I make best use of my time. It meant that every training session and every game was another step in the right direction. Without the goals in my mind I could have eased off, lost my way and lowered my standards.

In those early stages I only really knew about long-term or 'result' objectives such as scoring a certain number of goals, getting promoted or winning games. As I developed my knowledge I added 'process goals' that helped me along the way – and I got into the habit of setting little challenges to myself when I went into training, the gym or a game.

I found that, in some ways, process goals were better suited to me because I could control them. I had no power to control the performance of the opposition, my teammates or the referee, all of which could impact my ability to hit result goals. All I could do was play to my maximum and focus on my contribution. If I did that then I wouldn't be disappointed and my confidence wouldn't dip, regardless of the result.

In time I also realised that achieving goals of all types were the building blocks of my confidence. As each goal was achieved my faith in my ability grew along with the belief that I could hit future targets. Even now, a while after my football career has ended, I have a detailed set of written goals which I see every day. For instance I have a goal which states 'It's 8 August 2014 and I have started presenting my new sports show'.

In summary, I am a total convert and would be lost without them. They are as much a part of who I am as my flesh and blood. They have been an inspiration to me and have definitely improved my results. The mystery to me is why so few others adopt a similar approach. Apparently less than 3 per cent of the adult population have written down goals. Three per cent! That's just crazy and unfathomable, because if you don't know where you are trying to get to then you have no hope of getting there.

For me they are so helpful because they force me to ask myself fundamental questions, such as: what do I want from my life? The answers have never been purely about football. At any one time I have five or six goals on cards on the back of my bedroom door. Other people get to see them, but that doesn't embarrass me at all. I am just interested in creating an astonishing quality of life.

So while those goals have always included something on football they have happily existed alongside others such as going on a safari to Kenya, being able to play a song on the guitar at my sister's wedding, starting a degree before I am 30 and purchasing a house on the coast of Italy.

Currently I have a goal to climb Mount Kilimanjaro. I think that having goals outside football gives me more perspective and purpose, which helps to get me through the rough times. I think of Olympic athletes who train for years towards winning an Olympic medal. They wouldn't be able to endure all the pain and hard work if they didn't constantly have that end goal in mind. Certainly I believe goals should become an integral part of a footballer's toolkit to achieve peak performance. Research has demonstrated that high performers in all facets of life, as well as other mainstream sports – notably athletics, cycling, cricket and rugby – use them extensively. Yet in all my time in football I am aware of no more than five professionals who have had clear goals.

As a result this chapter is the only one in this book that does not have any role models at the end. I spoke to several people in the know, but no one could point out anyone within the game who has adopted a more structured approach than me to goal setting. I found that astonishing.

I guess that many opt out because they are afraid of a sense of failure, a blow to their self-esteem, if they fall short. To me that's woolly, weak thinking. I see failures as another form of feedback, just a blip along the journey. There are many examples of staggering innovations and human accomplishments that have been preceded by numerous setbacks.

Just to be clear – there are many footballers who are driven, dedicated and professional. Yet precisely what they want to achieve is unclear, unstructured and unwritten. I suppose vague ambitions are better than none, but over the years I have learned techniques for goal setting that brought them to life and helped them to become an even more powerful and positive force in my career.

One of the things that I quickly learned was that the more precise I made my goals the better. By that I mean the difference between, say, a target to 'play top-class football' and one that states 'play 50 games in the Premier League by my 23rd birthday'. The second is clearly a better target, because I would have known when I got there. The date would have focused my mind and I would have naturally worked harder, faster and with greater intensity as I approached the deadline.

By its very nature football is helpful in this regard. It's black and white in comparison with day-to-day life. You win, lose or draw; you either score a goal or you don't; you either get promoted, get relegated or stay in the same division. So setting specific and measurable goals shouldn't be too taxing.

In addition, for the goal to work I found that it needed to be challenging – something that stretched me and brought out the best in me. I think most of us set our sights too low because we are capable of far more than we think we are. Most of us can remember a task or target that felt impossible at an early stage of our development – swimming, riding a bike, driving a car – but now seems straightforward and everyday.

When I followed that framework I was able to create clear, constructive goals, and then I used the power of my imagination to help me achieve them. So if the aim was 'to score 20 goals by the end of the season' then I spent time in my bed or bath with my eyes shut visualising the ball hitting the back of the net, from all angles and distances, with head and both feet.

The premise behind this technique is that the brain can't tell the difference between real events and ones that are vividly imagined. So when, in my head, I imagined cutting in from the left wing and bending a curling shot into the top right-hand corner of the net the benefits were just the same when I was lying in my bed imagining it as when I did it for real on the training ground. In fact, with practice I could trigger the sensations associated with that run and shot just by pressing my thumb and forefinger together. They heightened my senses and released endorphins, which provide a sense of well-being. Both built up my muscle memory and nearly 40 per cent of my goals were scored in that way. No coincidence.

Visualisation also helped me to prepare for my Tottenham Hotspur home debut. I listened to a Paul McKenna tape when I was 19 years old and realised that he was on to something. He taught me to picture a scene and visualise the impact on my senses. So I would imagine walking out at White Hart Lane in front of a crowd of 35,000. I would see the bright lights, smell the damp grass and the Deep Heat, and hear the roars. The senses would be ramped up, more vivid and louder. I visualised feeling comfortable, positively excited, enjoying the experience, feeling at home.

Gerd Müller, the legendary goal-poacher from Bayern Munich and West Germany, was one of the early exponents. As long ago as the 1970s he used visualisation to help end rare goal droughts. More recently Wayne Rooney has also talked about how he rehearses upcoming matches in his head: 'I've done it since getting in the Everton team really. I've always asked the kit men what colour we're wearing, found out what colour the opponents are wearing and visualised scoring goals or good things happening in the game. I always do before every game, get good thoughts, good moments happening in the head. I do it the night before games, when I'm in bed.'

Finally, I validated that I really, really wanted to achieve the goal; that it would be an achievement that I would be proud of and give me great pleasure. I also made sure it was genuinely my goal rather than one that had been imposed upon me. I write that because I have seen it happen. Family and friends sometimes presume to know what's good for you. By accident they impose aspirations that you may not share. Or you may simply not have the drive and determination to achieve them. For instance, it's no good if they assume you want to play professional football when, deep down, you really want to travel the world and then run your own business. For me it all was about taking responsibility and being accountable for my actions – and if I didn't have a burning desire to achieve the goal then I needed to be brave enough to ditch it. I'd be unlikely to achieve it anyway if my heart wasn't in it.

Overall, I learned that when my goals were clear, challenging, desirable and realistic (though I'd add that exactly what is 'realistic' is entirely down to individual perception and many underestimate the full extent of their capabilities) then I had created conditions that gave clarity to my brain and provided me with the maximum possible chance of success.

As an example, when I was on the brink of the first team at Norwich City I went through a goal-setting process. I still have those sheets now and, as examples, I have reproduced them below.

GOAL NUMBER ONE

Outcome goal: To have scored five goals for the first team before the end of the season.
What this goal means to me: It means that I will be going a long way to becoming the number one striker by scoring five goals in 10 to 15 games.
My plan? Is to practise my finishing every day after training so when it comes to a game my mind and body will have repeated scoring a goal so many times that it will be natural.

GOAL NUMBER TWO

Outcome goal: To become first choice at Norwich until the end of the season and beyond.

What this goal means to me: It means that all my hard work and extra training will have paid off.

My plan? Is to continue playing in the first team until the end of the season, scoring at least five goals. This will give me a great opportunity to become first choice striker at Norwich City.

GOAL NUMBER THREE

Outcome goal: To increase my speed over 10m, 20m, 50m and 100m by the start of pre-season.

What this goal means to me: I think this extra advantage would give me more opportunities to get into goal scoring positions.

My plan? To practise my sprinting with a sprint/fitness coach, so I can improve my sprinting technique and overall increase my running speed.

After I had created these kinds of goals my conscious and subconscious mind locked on to them and worked on making them a reality. In fact, I found that the subconscious mind was incredibly powerful and because of that it didn't really matter if I knew how to reach the goal when I set it. I just needed to know that there was something that I genuinely wanted to achieve and then I would naturally gravitate towards it because I had primed my brain's filtering system to look out for opportunities to make progress.

What do I mean by that? Well, our senses are constantly bombarded with messages, communication, data and information. We cannot absorb it all, and nor do we want to. Like emails, we have a kind of spam filter that bins what's irrelevant before we have to deal with it. But by creating the goal we are alerting our personal spam filter to let relevant messages through.

An example: once I had finished playing football and started a media career one of my goals was to appear on Sky as a sports presenter. At the time I had no clue as to how I was going to make that my reality, but when I got an unexpected call from Stuart Jarrold, a journalist at Sky Sports, asking me for former Norwich City manager Mike Walker's phone number, a flashing light of opportunity went on in my brain. Sky told me that they were looking for Mike to be a studio guest at the Norwich versus Arsenal Premier League game. Actually Mike was overseas and unable to take up the offer, but because of my goal I half-jokingly mentioned to the journalist that I was interested and might be worth a go. The next day they rang me back and asked if I was available. Of course I was, and that match was a step on my journey towards one of my goals.

Seizing the opportunity to appear on Sky Sports – here with Dave Jones and Alan Smith. I am relishing my increasing media roles.

Finally, a word of caution. I found that one of the few drawbacks with goals is the hangover that can occur after they have been achieved. I've mentioned elsewhere in this book what happened after I made my debut for Tottenham Hotspur. That debut saw the fulfilment of a goal that had existed for me from the age of eight or nine through to 19 when I achieved it. It was a massive highlight, and what happened afterwards? I went into celebration mode – which would have been justified for a weekend but not for a whole summer – and lost all my focus and intensity because there was no longer a goal to focus my energies upon.

Of course the smart people set themselves short-, medium- and long-term goals, and once they have achieved one goal they waste little time in turning their attention to the next. Think of Sir Alex Ferguson. He enjoys success, then moves on and looks to the next challenge.

What advice would I give to young footballers who read these words and are inspired to set out their goals? What kind of goal would I suggest? Well, one thing is for certain: I don't want to set goals for others to achieve. As I suggested before, that seldom works. The whole point is that they need to be defined by the person. For me to place my goals on someone else would be effectively to place my dreams, my expectations and my ambitions on to someone else when they may have no interest in achieving them. That does happen, often with parents placing their dreams on to their children, and it normally doesn't work out too well because the child does not have the passion and drive to achieve them.

What will help with the process of setting goals is to sit down and take stock of where your life is – what I describe as your 'clear and current reality'. Consider all the aspects of your life, not just football. Include topic areas such as hobbies, money, fitness/health, relationships, spirituality and education, and rate yourself with a score out of 10. That will give you an idea of what's going well and help you to pick out maybe three areas to focus on.

When a young player is uncertain over their life goals it raises alarm bells for me. If they don't know what they want, that is a clear indication of lack of focus and passion, and if they get to their early teens and are not clear on their goals I might be discouraging them from getting into professional football. By that age if you are uncertain whether you want to be a professional footballer then it's probably a good indication that it's not the career for you. I would advise that you work on your education and go and get an apprenticeship. That could save a lot of tears down the line.

Nowadays there are very few footballers that make it who are not moving through the academies at an early age or don't have the clear, driven goal to play professional football. Kids are getting coached earlier and earlier, drilled into good habits, and the smart ones are entirely focused on what they want to achieve. There may be some who don't emerge from formal structures and still make it, but that is very rare and will become even rarer.

KEY MESSAGES

Most high achievers, in all walks of life, have specific and challenging goals with associated timelines in mind. They should inspire us and give us direction and purpose.

Goals are massively important to what we achieve because they give clarity and a challenge to our brain, directing our conscious and subconscious thinking. This can be supported by visualisation, which is a great way of practising and building muscle memory because the subconscious can't tell the difference between real and vividly imagined events.

Once we are clear on what we want to achieve then we can create an action plan on how to achieve and then start imagining success. However, when setting a goal, don't get bogged down in how you are going to achieve it and the potential barriers and obstacles in the way. It is more important for us to know where we want to go than how we are going to get there.

LESSON FOUR

THINK ABOUT THINKING

One of the key lessons that I learned during my football career was that I needed to work on the way that I thought about things. Actually I found that what I thought about wasn't as important as the way that I thought about it. Confused? I simply mean that I worked out that I had a choice in how I reacted to events and that it was in my interests to choose an option that gave me the kind of emotions that I wanted. Still confused? Well, here are two scenarios to consider. How would you have reacted to these events?

SCENARIO 1

You play in the Championship Play-Off final at Cardiff's Millennium Stadium in front of 75,000 fans. The winning team will be promoted to the Premiership and will receive an estimated £30 million. Success will also have a significant impact on your career because it opens up the possibility of playing at the highest possible level in English football, pitting your skills against household names every week.

After 90 minutes the match is goalless. In the first minute of extra time your team scores, but the lead only lasts nine minutes. After 120 minutes it's still 1–1, and so it is decided by penalties, where your team loses 4–2. You watch the opposition players and fans celebrate as your teammates slump to the ground, many in tears.

How would you feel? How would you react?

SCENARIO 2

You have recently taken over a football club playing in League One. They were struggling before your appointment, but you have improved their fortunes, lifting them up towards the top of the table. One Monday night you travel to play the strongest opposition in the league on their home ground in a hostile atmosphere. But you match them – pass for pass, shot for shot, through 90 minutes. The score is 1–1 when, with the last action of the game, your young goalkeeper scuffs a goal kick straight to their centre-forward, who races through, unchallenged, to score.

Disconsolate, your team troops off the pitch and into the dressing room.

How would you feel? How would you react?

The player in 'Scenario 1' was me and the match was the 2001/2002 Championship Play-Off final between Norwich City and Birmingham City.

As we were walking round the pitch after the game I saw grown men crying. But I wasn't; quite the reverse. I was walking round with a smile on my face. Although I desperately wanted to win, my overriding emotion was one of gratitude that I'd had the opportunity to play the game that I love in the wonderful Millennium Stadium in front of 75,000 fans and a global audience of millions. What an experience – one that I will always remember.

Was I taking defeat too lightly? I don't think so. I gave everything to get us promoted. In all I played 49 games that season, scoring 10 goals, including four in the run-up to the end of season when we scraped into the play-offs. And I knew that I had played really well in the play-off final. In short, I was confident that I'd done as much as anyone to get us so close. No one could question my desire or commitment.

So I chose to relish the experience and feel grateful for it, even in defeat. It was no coincidence that rather than feeling depressed and down through the summer I was able to bounce back quickly, and the next season I was top scorer at the club.

The second scenario was the League One match between Leeds United and Norwich City on Monday 19 October 2009. The Norwich manager was Paul Lambert and it was his first defeat since taking over. I was an unused substitute that night.

Because we'd lost, the players trooped into the dressing room with the perception that it had been a terrible game. They were gutted to have lost to rivals for promotion and that feeling was multiplied because the winning goal was with the last kick of the game. Of course no one felt worse than the young goalkeeper, Fraser Forster, whose individual error had led to the goal.

So how the did the manager react? In the dressing room Paul Lambert's body language and words to the team were upbeat and positive. He said 'you may have lost but look at how well you played. You've come to Elland Road, one of the hardest grounds in the country to go to and you've played so well. We made plenty of chances, we scored a good goal and should have definitely won the game. We're going to bounce back next week.' In front of the rest of the team he told Fraser Forster what a great young goalkeeper he was and what a top-class goalkeeper he was going to become.

Because of the result the team may have been expecting criticism, even some 'hairdryer' treatment, but Lambert's words and demeanour immediately lifted the mood – and this was particularly apparent with Fraser. You could see him sit up and immediately feel better about himself. This encouraged him to come into training the next week feeling in good spirits, and that allowed him to train well.

Within minutes of the final whistle, while we were still in the dressing room at Elland Road, we had moved on and started our preparation for the next game. That preparation was physical – through ice baths, hydration, food and the like – but also mental. Lambert helped us to put the Leeds match behind us, still feel good about it, and have a greater determination to win the next one, which we did. In fact we then embarked on a seven-match unbeaten run. It sounds obvious, but the longer you spend dwelling on defeat, the less time you have to prepare for the next match.

I guess some in the team may have been surprised by Lambert's response. There is a culture in football that after a defeat players are automatically criticised and sometimes they get slaughtered. Often there is an inquest, with scapegoats identified and everyone made to feel they need to walk around for days with a miserable look on their face to show how much they care. But I don't think that works. To create that kind of environment, to my mind, is stupid management.

Don't be misled by this story. Paul Lambert is not a soft, happy-clappy man-manager. He has the highest standards of anyone I've ever seen. His thinking and focus on winning games is extraordinary. I've never seen anything like it. His one and only aim, in every minute of every day, is to win, and there's no let-up. Nor would I describe him as a good loser. He has no favourites and if someone is out of line they will soon know it.

However, he has the respect of the players, not least because of his track record in the game. He played at the highest level and won the biggest prizes, representing Scotland, Celtic and Borussia Dortmund, with whom he won the Champions League. So he knows what is needed to become a winner and leads by example.

I think that his experience in Germany was critical. You wouldn't say that the German mentality is the most happy-go-lucky, but they are the smartest people when it comes to football because all they are thinking about is: How are we going to win the next game? How are we going to improve? What training session do we need to toughen us up physically so that in six months' time we'll still be fit enough to keep performing?

When Lambert talks, people listen, so he is able to turn everything, even what might be seen by some as negative events, into a positive, a challenge.

Crucially, he focuses on the performance and the process more than the results. By that I mean that he is looking for whether the players have prepared well and whether they were committed, hard-working and following his instructions more than the result of the game.

While he knows that football is a results-driven business, he also knows that the process is even more important, because if his team keeps doing all the right things then they will play to their full potential and the results will follow. In the short term results can be skewed by things you can't control – opposition brilliance, refereeing decisions, and so on – and if the only focus is on results then it can be difficult to gauge how you are doing.

That night in Leeds he wanted to win but was happy with the performance. So he picked people up, told them how good they were and went through all the good things they had done in the game. Fraser Forster, for instance, is a conscientious young man who had prepared properly for the game and had probably done 30 things well that evening: made good saves, held crosses, kicked consistently. But he made one, high-profile mistake. So the choice for the manager was what he opted to focus on. It wasn't sweeping the mistake under the carpet but saying okay, let's improve on that next time.

I think the critical point that I'm making from both these scenarios – me at the play-off final and Paul Lambert after defeat at Leeds – is the same, and it's this: we have a choice in what we think about and how we think, and therefore we have a choice in how we react to what may be perceived as setbacks. The only place that events have meaning is in our heads. Each event is neutral, neither good nor bad, and how it is perceived is down to how we decide to interpret it. Not everyone gives every event the same meaning.

With practice I conditioned myself to choose how I thought about things. A lot of people believe that their ways of thinking are derived from their past, people around them and their environment. In fact that is not the case. They have an influence, but they are not the crucial factors.

Consider this: two youngsters get released from a football club at 14 years old. One decides that this rejection means he is not good enough and gives up on his dreams; the other is motivated to go and prove the club wrong.

Or listen to this story about twin brothers: their father is abusive, unemployed and an alcoholic. The twins grow up. One also becomes abusive, unemployed and an alcoholic; the other has a good job, lovely spouse and happy family. They were asked 'how did you turn out that way?' And they both answered the same way: 'with a dad like that how else could you turn out?'

Why do some people have the most terrible things happen to them in their lives and still have a smile on their face, whereas others appear to have an abundance of everything – money in the bank, good job – but are utterly miserable? Why is that?

I learned that our thinking patterns drive every emotion that we have. I worked hard to become a more constructive thinker because it made me more likely to have positive emotions, and be more creative, more determined and more motivated.

We create our emotions every single day, and there are implications and consequences of thinking positively or negatively. Research has shown just how much optimists outperform pessimists. Optimists take on new challenges, are enthusiastic and passionate, and are not diverted when things go wrong, whereas pessimists stop at the first setback. So, over time and with practice, I made progress in rewiring my thinking patterns to help me to become the best footballer that I could be.

ROLE MODEL

When it comes to thinking in constructive ways my mind is drawn to Steven Gerrard, one of the most complete Premier League players over the last 20 years, described to me by a teammate as 'the most mentally strong professional I have played with'.

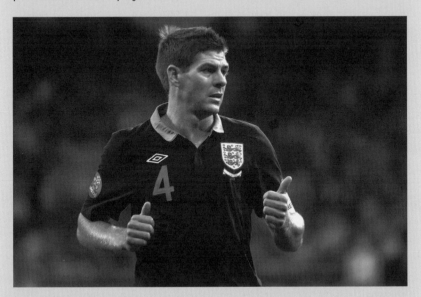

Steven Gerrard, England's captain: a leader through actions as much as words and incredibly mentally resilient.

Gerrard is not a motivator through long and wordy speeches to teammates. But he doesn't need to be. We can see all we need to see about his attitude from his performances on the pitch and the way that he has been the driving force behind his beloved Liverpool – and England too – on so many occasions.

Of course the most obvious example of Gerrard at his inspirational best came in the 2005 Champions League final in Istanbul against AC Milan. At half time Liverpool were 3–0 down and torn to pieces. The match seemed done and dusted.

Within that Liverpool dressing room at half time some would have been mentally shot to pieces. Some would have wanted the match to be over as quickly as possible so they could skulk out of the stadium, away from the scene of the embarrassment. But at times like that the cream rises to the top. Liverpool needed leaders who reveal their full worth in adversity and uncover new depths of courage and strength that lesser mortals simply don't have.

Gerrard, as so often for Liverpool, was that leader, and the key was not what he thought about but the way that he thought about it. Everyone in that dressing room was 'thinking' about the fact that they were getting hammered in front of a global audience in one of the most important matches that they would ever play in. So there were no differences there. What was different was the way that Gerrard chose to view the 0–3 scoreline as an opportunity to make history rather than crawl into a hole. He didn't accept failure.

His mentality was to say 'this is the Champions League final. Very few players make it to this level and I'm not going down without a fight.' Incidentally I'm sure that Jamie Carragher, another leader in the dressing room, would have been thinking the same way.

Gerrard came out of that dressing room and took the fight to Milan. Eight minutes after half time he looped a header into their net and hurried back to the centre circle, sensing an opportunity, a possible turning point. A minute later it was 2–3, and six minutes after that Gerrard burst into the penalty box again and was pulled down as he was poised to score. Xabi Alonso had his penalty saved but followed up to score with the rebound. On the hour mark it became 3–3. Liverpool went on to win 3–2 on penalties after extra time to complete a memorable comeback.

Of course, it is too easy to say that the phenomenon of Liverpool in Istanbul was entirely down to Steven Gerrard's mental strength and desire to win. In truth, there were many other reasons: Milan's complacency, Dudek's goalkeeping, Carragher's last-ditch tackles, the loyal support of the Liverpool fans and, above all, the early goal in the second half that gave them hope. But, for me, it can all be traced back to Gerrard's will and belief, and the way he saw the half-time scoreline as a challenge.

Nor is it a one-off. Gerrard will always look for the positives. Amazingly, he drove Liverpool forward again in the FA Cup final a year later against West Ham. This time they were two down after 28 minutes, but again they came back and Gerrard scored equalisers to make it 2–2 and then 3–3. The latter was an unstoppable low shot from 35 yards in the last minute of the game after he had been struggling with cramp and operating at about 20 per cent of his normal capabilities. It's what great players do, and by then Gerrard had become a great player. He also scored in the penalty shoot-out as Liverpool went on to win the FA Cup.

His capacity to turn what many might see as negatives into challenges was also shown with the captaincy of the England national team. He has been treated in an erratic way by various managers. When he has been given the captain's armband it has seemed almost grudging – and he has also had it taken away. Yet he has dealt with that frustration well, never coming out in the media and complaining, and eventually he showed what a good captain he is during the 2012 European Championships when he led by example and was by far England's best player.

Not every footballer plays in high-profile cup finals or captains his country. But the principle of consciously choosing to think constructively in difficult circumstances works at several levels. I work with a lot of young players who are affected when they make a mistake such as giving the ball away or missing a chance in front of goal. They dwell on the mistake, and if it's a glaring one it can ruin their performance for the rest of the game.

Yet mistakes are part and parcel of football. Every player makes them. It's nearly impossible to pass every ball to a teammate, score every chance and have the perfect game. So when a misplaced pass or missed opportunity occurs players do best to put it behind them immediately. Steven Gerrard does that. Within a nanosecond he has moved on as if it hadn't happened. Through this kind of constructive thinking he has consistently proven down the years – by actions more than words – that he represents a great role model to follow.

KEY MESSAGES

What you think about isn't as important as the way you think about what you think about! With practice and discipline it is possible to change thinking patterns to our benefit.

Every event is neutral. What is more important is the way that we react and, with practice, we can condition ourselves to react in more constructive, helpful ways so that we get more of what we want.

Thinking patterns drive our emotions, and they in turn drive our behaviour, habits and our results. So if we think more constructively we are also likely to achieve better results.

LESSON FIVE

FOCUS ON SUCCESS –
TO GET MORE OUT OF IT

The best way for me to explain focus in football is to use a true story that actually comes from the golf course and involves my dad. A couple of years ago I was playing golf with him on a wet day in Northern Ireland. We reached the par-four 16th hole, and after two straight drives we were left with second shots of around 130 yards in length. Looking to help me, he warned that there was a bunker to the right-hand, of the green that was well worth avoiding, and also one on the left.

His guidance set off a few alarm bells for me and I asked where he was aiming to hit the ball. He said, as you might expect, 'onto the green, close to the hole'. So I asked him why, if that was the case, he was talking about the bunkers? Why not just focus on where he wanted to hit it, aim for and expect success, and put the ball as close to the pin as possible?

I explained a bit more about what I had learned about the working of the brain and he looked at me as if to say 'that seems pretty logical, that makes sense'. Then he hit an eight-iron that travelled straight as a dye through the rain, bounced once and went straight into the hole. We were going mental, high-fiving and laughing.

I don't claim to take all the credit for my Dad's eagle or guarantee that having access to this theory will lead you to such immediate sporting success. But it did highlight the benefits of focusing on what you want to happen, rather than what you are trying to avoid. As a caveat to this story, my dad has been playing golf for over 30 years now, and since this incident he has shot three holes-in-one within 18 months! Maybe that's just a coincidence …

A lot of people in the game talk endlessly about focus. Managers are always 'focusing on the next game' or urging their team to 'keep its focus'. But most don't understand the concept. The brain is always focusing on something. That's not the problem. It does it quite naturally. The challenge is to focus it in a constructive and helpful direction.

What I explained to my dad was what I had learned from my mentor Gavin Drake – that the brain has three main ways in which it can be focused (more about his work later in this chapter):

- it can expect to fail;
- it can try not to fail; or
- it can expect to succeed.

Gavin had explained to me that when we 'focus' we should be channelling our energy into what we want to happen with an expectation of achieving that aim. The brain works 'teleologically', which means that it will lock on to and help you to achieve whatever you focus on, and quite naturally, you will gravitate in that direction.

This works to your advantage when you focus on something positive. However, quite the reverse is also true. That's because the brain has a blind spot when it comes to negatives. It doesn't 'do a don't' – in other words, it ignores the negatives within a sentence.

In the phrase 'I hope I don't miss the penalty' the brain cannot compute the 'don't', so it zones in on helping you to do exactly what you want to avoid. If you think 'I hope I don't get nervous', guess what will happen? You're more likely to get nervous. If you think 'I hope I don't mess up today', guess what will happen?

Understanding this concept encouraged a massive leap forward in my thinking. I understood how damaging it was to allow myself to dwell on what might go wrong, and I began to condition myself to be more constructive. How did I do that? Well, there was no magic formula – there never is – I just got better through consciously becoming aware of when my focus had become negative and unhelpful. When that happened I replaced it with more purposeful habits. With repetition, after a while it became more natural and the change definitely made me a better player.

All of this may seem pretty obvious, but while it is common sense it is most definitely not common practice. Football managers, in particular, waste a lot of time telling their players what they don't want them to do. This is misguided, because if you are going into games fearing defeat or trying not to get beaten then the focus is all wrong.

At the time of writing Spain are the current reigning world and European champions, having won the 2010 FIFA World Cup and the 2008 and 2012 UEFA European Football Championships, and have also been top of the FIFA World Rankings for several years.

It is easy to forget that for decades they were underperformers in international football. At major tournament after major tournament they failed to deliver the results that their talent demanded. They buckled under the pressure, and I think that was all about mindset. As the failures built through the 1990s and much of the 2000s, the players went into key matches hoping *not* to be the latest squad to underdeliver. They were trying *not* to lose, *not* to mess up. Eventually the sheer weight of quality within the team led to victory in the Euros in 2008, and once the psychological shackles were broken their confidence and expectation of success increased, leading to World Cup glory in South Africa in 2010.

Think, too, of England in penalty shoot-outs. What sort of mentality do the penalty takers have? Are they expecting to score, or hoping not to miss? Most pray that they don't become the next one in the long list of fall guys started by Stuart Pearce and Chris Waddle in Italy in 1990. Not a constructive mindset. All of England's penalty takers have been top, top footballers. Most can execute a pinpoint pass while running at speed, off balance, over 50 yards, but when it comes to the penalty kick with the eyes of the world upon them the fear factor kicks in. They overthink and become technical and mindful of the process. That compromises their ability to perform.

Does the nation expect England to win in a penalty shoot-out? No, not a chance. They expect to lose – and so do most of the players. It's a well-known truism: England loses in penalty shoot-outs. It will take a shift in mindset and a win against a nation who takes an even worse set of penalties than England to begin to make a psychological breakthrough.

It would help if they had more players with the self-assurance of one of my teammates at Tottenham, Teddy Sheringham. Teddy successfully took a penalty in the high-pressure shoot-out against Germany in the Euro 96 semi-final. I asked him about it and he said 'yeah, I knew I was going to score'. But I said 'you put it right in the very top corner of the goal, it wasn't even a safe penalty'. And he said 'yeah, I just knew I was going to score'. For him it was never in doubt. But Sheringham was unusual in that he just had an unbreakable self-belief and would back himself against anyone or anything.

Closer to home, I think back to when I was with Norwich City in the Premiership in the 2004/2005 season. Our whole focus that year was on not getting relegated. We knew that we were in the big league; we knew that there were many stronger, richer teams around us; and we knew that if we could consolidate for a season or two then we would be able to progress. Within the club, the whole focus was on not getting relegated. Of course, the target was a negative – based around something that we didn't want to happen. Worse, there was an implied belief within the management that the best we could achieve was 17th place. That was the height of our ambition, and the goal suggested that this was only achievable if we played to our full potential. That didn't give us much room for manoeuvre. If our performance standards fell at all then we would slip back into the relegation zone in 18th, 19th or 20th place. How much better would it have been if we had focused on getting into the top 10 or winning all our home games? We would have taken a completely different mentality into each match.

Although it was a team target, it also affected individuals, because that was all that people talked about, and it seeped into our self-image, our ways of thinking and the general culture within the club. We were downbeat and fearful. Although it's always going to be a challenge for promoted teams, as professionals we should have been aiming higher, enjoying the experience, looking to create some shocks and headlines, upping our game.

At the time we simply didn't know about this stuff. No one had educated us and we were misguided. All our efforts and hard work, commitment and dedication were futile because it was directed towards *not* getting relegated, *not* losing games, *not* getting thrashed at the likes of Old Trafford, Stamford Bridge and Anfield. We were running in an easterly direction looking for a sunset. Little wonder that it took us until 20 November to win a game and we were in the bottom three for pretty much all of the season.

In the January 2005 transfer window we bought centre-forward Dean Ashton from Crewe for £3 million, and he made a massive impact because he was a genuine talent and in the habit of thinking in a more constructive way. He came into our dressing room and culture untainted by a negative mindset. He'd been a prolific scorer at Crewe – scoring 20 goals in the first half of the season – and his confidence was sky high.

He relished the challenge of the Premier League and his whole manner suggested that he expected to do well. He wasn't at all cocky, but he had a confidence about him that said 'I'm going to score goals, I'm going to cause defenders problems'. Allied to that mindset was a natural ability to score out of nothing. Ashton was a breath of fresh air, and his attitude kick-started everyone else, refocusing us.

He scored seven Premiership goals during the rest of the season, making a name for himself, and we rallied towards the spring, notably beating Manchester United. But it was too little too late, and we got relegated at Fulham on the last day of the season. Would it have been different if Ashton had been with us from the start of the season? Possibly, but perhaps he would have been influenced and dragged down by our ways of thinking, and might not have had the same impact.

That possibility became more apparent as we struggled to adapt to life back in the Championship. There was a definite hangover and we underperformed, Ashton included. Self-esteem was low; we took only three points from our first six games, and by early December we were still in the doldrums.

Fortunately our manager, Nigel Worthington, brought in Gavin Drake, a sports psychologist, to work with us. Drake was another much-needed breath of fresh air and some of his concepts are featured within this book. He explained how our thinking drives our emotions, and that emotions lead to actions, behaviours, habits and ultimately results. He explained focus theory and the importance of pointing our thinking in the right direction so that we made good use of our undoubtedly strong work ethic.

He had a big impact on Dean Ashton, and even more so on me, so much so that I am still gaining benefit several years on now that I have finished playing. Best of all, the short-term impact on the team was immediate and startling. In the next game we were 1–0 down to Crewe at half time before I scored two in the second half to secure a victory. I scored four more in the next seven games, and the team won five on the spin, including a win over Southampton when Ashton scored a hat-trick.

The trick in focusing my thinking was to train and condition myself. There is no great secret and it's available to all of us. Indeed the more I do it, the more I do it – and I have no doubt that I have enjoyed benefits, not least in how I deal with stress, pressure and nerves.

Some nerves before a match are inevitable and, actually, all part of the build-up of adrenalin needed to perform at your best. Partly because I got into some strong thinking habits, my dominant emotions before a game were excitement and anticipation rather than anxiety or being weighed down by pressure. I tend to side with one of my managers who, in a team-talk before an important match, said 'what pressure?' He said that people who are on the front line of wars, save lives in hospitals or have four kids at home and lose their jobs know what pressure is. Not footballers that kick a ball around and try to win a game.

I agree. At times football seems to be the most important thing in the world – and, as a professional, you need to attach importance to it. Yet it is just a game, and just occasionally the realities of life kick in and highlight this.

For me the starkest example came after the first leg of the Championship Play-Off semi-final at Carrow Road. We beat Wolverhampton Wanderers 3–1 and I scored. It was contested in a great atmosphere and I played really well. I left the ground after the match on a high, my adrenalin pumping with a post-win buzz.

As I drove home I went down a side street with cars parked down both sides. From nowhere a little wee girl broke away from her family and ran straight on to the road and into my path. I had no time to stop. I was only travelling at 20 miles per hour, but the girl was knocked to the ground and lay motionless on the road in front of my car.

While her family rushed to her aid, I sat in the car in a cold sweat, paralysed with shock and fear. What had I done? It was, without doubt, the worst moment of my life. All I could think about was what I had done to this very young girl. In time, the police and ambulance service arrived and took statements. The girl was taken to hospital as I remained frozen and numb, devastated and heartbroken, even though I knew there was nothing I could have done to avoid the collision.

That night I went to the cathedral and prayed for the girl to recover, with any thoughts of a now irrelevant game of football long gone. Eventually I phoned my family and, of course, they wanted to talk about the thrilling match they had just watched me play in on television. But I wasn't interested. Two days later I was called by the police and informed that the girl had a broken collarbone and was on the road to recovery. Even though the injury was serious it could have been so much worse, and the news came as a great relief. Even so, I played in the second leg of the semi-final on autopilot. My thoughts were with her, and although I put in a professional shift and played well I was not in the ideal frame of mind and didn't enjoy the fact that we reached the play-off final.

Just to be clear – I am not seeking to be the hero of this story. Nor do I deserve sympathy. This was a horrific moment in the lives of the girl and her family, and her full recovery is the only good to come out of it. I only share the memory in this book because it highlights, and helped me to understand, that football is only important at a basic level. Although it is a pastime that gives pleasure to millions, its importance should not be compared with the harsher incidents of 'real' life. And so when we attribute pressure to activities related to sport we should all bear that in mind.

That said, I appreciate that although we can probably all see the logic in that argument, it doesn't mean that some footballers don't suffer excessive nerves and stress, which can impair performance and their enjoyment of the footballing experience. For some it even leads to depression.

I learned that to avoid being affected by nerves there was no point telling myself *not* to be nervous. I needed to fill my thoughts with more positive thinking, whether that was winning, scoring, playing my best or simply enjoying the experience. That deprived my brain of the space for unhelpful thoughts. Even though it doesn't sound like a huge difference it was actually a completely different psychological attitude. A winner's mentality is fuelled by genuinely strong, effective and helpful thought patterns. It's not airy-fairy, pink and fluffy. It's not psychobabble or mumbo-jumbo. By improving in this area I was still aware of issues and challenges; I just didn't focus on them to the same degree, and my on-pitch performances inevitably improved.

In doing so I was emulating the best of the best. In any walk of life, any sport, the highest performers have conditioned themselves to zone in on success. In tennis do you think the likes of Djokovic, Nadal and Federer are trying not to lose the match? No, they know and believe that they are going to win and they want to beat their opponent hard. The elite performers focus on what they want to achieve, so it's no coincidence that they become the best of the best.

ROLE MODELS

In football it is easy to find elite performers whose mindset and attitude are entirely pointed towards success and winning – and it is easiest to identify in those who have finished their career as a footballer and moved into management. In this way we get more access to their personalities so that the will and drive to win is more evident.

I've mentioned several times in this chapter, and the book as a whole, my admiration for Paul Lambert. He was a winner as a player and he is a winner as a manager. He is totally single-minded and has no time for self-doubt or negative thinking. I once interviewed him and asked him what he wanted to achieve as a manager. Without hesitation, he said 'to win trophies'. Having that clear goal drives the way he works, and it's very clear that he is only in football for that reason. So I have no doubt that some day he will be at a really top club where he has the opportunity to regularly be in contention for the top honours in British and European football.

Maybe it's a Scottish or Glaswegian trait, but I see the same mindset in another manager, Sir Alex Ferguson. Of course Ferguson has already achieved all that Lambert aspires to achieve. He has been a winner at Manchester United for years now, and it's his love of winning that has kept him going when he has every right to retire and reflect on his many successes. He must be the greatest football manager who has ever lived, although I'd also like to compliment one of Ferguson's chief adversaries over the past 15 years, Arsène Wenger.

Wenger works on a smaller budget, but to get Arsenal into the Champions League so regularly over that period is a glowing endorsement of his managerial abilities. Wenger has not been competing on a level playing field against the riches of Manchester United and, more recently, Chelsea and Manchester City. Yet he has constructed a blueprint that has put strong foundations in place.

Of course the likes of Wenger and Ferguson inevitably have a big impact on the players that play for them, and there have been several stand-out players in the United team that have grown up in a culture where everything is so focused on success and winning that it has become second nature.

Arsène Wenger knows the game inside out. He is a winner who has consistently led Arsenal into the Champions League.

Gary Neville had that fire and passion to succeed, and in a less vocal way Paul Scholes was a winner to his core, but perhaps Roy Keane was the most obvious example of that. He found it difficult to understand and cope when those around him didn't share his obsessive pursuit of victory. That's why Sir Alex Ferguson and Keane made such a great team as manager and captain at Manchester United. They were totally in synch with their expectations of the players. Their base requirements were the same and they made a powerful combination that allowed no let-up from anyone.

Gary Doherty – who played with me at Norwich and with Roy Keane for the Republic of Ireland – told me that in every single practice session on international duty the team with Keane always won. That tells us everything we need to know about the man. He just had such a relentless desire to win that it could never be satisfied. Because of that desire he got the best out of others, dragging them up to his own Olympian standards. If they fell short he was on to them: cajoling, encouraging, shouting.

I should add that Keane provided much more than just a competitive nature to the teams he played for. He was a great all-round footballer: a ferocious tackler, an underrated passer of the ball – at least as good as his much-admired teammate Paul Scholes – and his energy to get around the whole pitch and influence play was awesome. He could dominate a game single-handedly.

Yet despite Keane's excellence, of all those long-standing Manchester United veterans it is Ryan Giggs who comes to my mind as the best current example of someone who has directed his thinking towards long-term success. That's proven by his amazing list of achievements in the game:

- Club record for competitive appearances
- Over 1000 senior appearances (club and international)
- Two Champions League winner's medals
- 12 Premier League winner's medals
- Four FA Cup winner's medals
- Three League Cup winner's medals

Giggs is another who would be quite entitled to sit back and rest on his laurels but, like Ferguson, he has never lost his appetite for the game. Despite 20 years at Manchester United he just keeps moving forward, still up for the next test and hungry for success. He never looks back and dwells, never focuses on negatives. For him it is all about the next challenge – all about success, all about winning. When you think in that way you naturally gravitate towards whatever is required to help you achieve those things.

Giggs has been smart enough to know that if he wants to win he must be willing to change and reinvent himself, a trait that added years to his career. He started as a lightning-fast left-winger – a fantastic dribbler and crosser of the ball with an eye for goal, and probably one of the best Premier League players ever. As he lost that edge of speed he moved in behind the front two where he still displayed his attacking ability and could pick out and play a killer pass. Then, as he grew older and lost the running power of the youngsters, he moved into the centre of midfield and even played a Champions League final in that role. By then he had become a real scholar of the game; he just understood it, like his teammate Paul Scholes. All the time he just knew where players should be.

Giggs has been a driving force behind United's success over the years, and that inner drive and will to win has helped him to be self-motivated enough to consistently deliver enthusiastic, energetic performances – something that cannot be taken for granted after playing professional football for so long.

KEY MESSAGES

Focus is one of the most important aspects in psychology. The highest performers in all walks of life are in the habit of focusing constructively. Because their focus is directed towards an expectation of success, it helps them to achieve more and deal more effectively with what others may perceive to be stress, pressure and nerves.

There are three main ways to focus – expect to fail, try not to fail, expect to succeed – and regardless of how we focus, the brain locks on to this and tries to helps us to achieve it.

The achievement of personal excellence and the expectation of success are great habits to get into. The more excellence and success we have, the more we want and expect it.

LESSON SIX

MEET ADVERSITY WITH STRENGTH

As my career developed it became crystal clear to me that in the modern game it is more important to have mental strength than physical strength. What I needed was the resilience to cope with the inevitable challenges to my state of mind, whether that was dealing with rejection, injuries, poor performance or criticism from managers, other players, fans, my family and, not least, myself.

Even when I was totally focused and my attitude was spot on there were still times when it all went wrong, when nothing worked no matter what I tried. That's simply the nature of football, not to mention day-to-day life. And every time I had one of those days when my mental strength was challenged, would I wilt like a little flower or rise to the challenge?

The fragile flowers allow adversity to beat them and they inevitably fall by the wayside. Put bluntly, there is not one chance in a hundred that I could have sustained a long-term career path if I had been easily diverted off course by setbacks and challenges – and, as for any footballer, they were a constant if unwanted companion.

It might be helpful to give you an extensive tour of the blips that I met along my career path and explain how I improved in dealing with them through a growing maturity and, more importantly, the development of the kind of mental skills that I have been outlining in this book.

You'll see as we go through them that I needed each and every one of the tools in my psychological toolkit – a strong self-image, focusing on success, taking personal responsibility for my thinking, choosing to see the upsides in challenging circumstances and an unending desire to achieve my personal goals – at one time or another. My career probably contained fewer setbacks than most, yet logging them for this book has reminded me that I could easily have been beaten by them and given up.

In fact I could have given up when I was in my teens. When I was young and inexperienced, the blows hit me harder and I took longer to recover from them. A trial for Northern Ireland's under-15 squad provided my first sour taste of rejection. Up until then all had gone to plan. I had signed schoolboy terms with Tottenham and been the best player in pretty much every team I had played in, suitably lavished with praise and the winner of cups and trophies.

Although I got down to a short-list of 30 boys for the international squad, when the list of those who had made it to the next stage of the selection process was read out my name was missing. It was a harsh lesson that not everything would fall into my lap, and I took it pretty hard. As my parents drove me back to our home in West Belfast I was distraught and in tears. For a while it consumed my thoughts, not least because I thought the failure was down to my lack of height. At that stage I was no more than five feet tall, competing against some boys who were much more physically advanced in their development: a foot taller, faster, quicker and stronger. It was a pretty big worry and I saw it as a massive stumbling block for my chances of a career in the game. I was keen to work hard to improve, but there was nothing I could do about my genes. I remember saying 'what chance do I have?'

Although it felt awful at the time, and I moped for quite a while, the fact that I was with Tottenham helped spur me on, and they eventually offered me a one-year contract, which was followed by a three-year one. However, through injuries, limited opportunities and the views of the manager George Graham I suffered rejection a second time and was released by the club at the age of 21.

Again, it seemed to be about my lack of height rather than ability. George had a preconception that he wanted players of six foot one, six foot two in his side. He put physical attributes above the technical. I was slight and five foot six – so he wasn't looking at me even though I was top scorer in the reserves.

I knocked on his door, pushing for a place, and he broke the news to me: 'I just don't think you're good enough for the Premier League. You're too small. You'd better start looking for another club.' I was angry that he dismissed me because of my size because I saw other small players doing well in the Premier League who were technically good – and I knew that I was technically better than many. I knew there was a place for me somewhere, but clearly it wasn't going to be with George Graham.

In fact, coming out of that meeting I felt really determined. I thought 'no, no you're wrong. I can do it and I'm going to show you and prove to myself that I can do it.' After that I had a burning passion and belief. For me, that rejection turned things around and gave me a purpose. So even within those years my approach to setbacks – and to be leaving a club of Tottenham's stature was obviously a body blow – had already developed. Instead of feeling sorry for myself and moping, I moved fairly quickly through anger into a resolution to bounce back. I did so with Norwich City, then in the Championship, who offered me a contract. As I edged closer and closer to their first team I encountered my next challenge, one that I wouldn't have seen coming in a million years.

Malky MacKay is now a really good friend. I really like him, we speak all the time and I take great pleasure in his success as an up-and-coming football manager. However, when I broke into the first-team squad at the club he caused me some stress because he absolutely killed me with his verbals in the dressing room.

Malky has a big personality. He's witty, clever and he can cut you down in no time. He certainly gave me both barrels. I was young and didn't have any comebacks. To me it felt like I was getting a torrent of abuse, and others like Craig Fleming were also not averse to adding their own funny but caustic comments. In the end I got really down about it. I felt it was personal, and didn't understand why it was never ending. I was just like a punchbag with nothing to throw back at them and no comprehension of why I was getting picked on. It affected my performance on the pitch and my happiness off the pitch.

I went to my dad for advice. Typically he suggested – as he was not averse to a scrap – that I should hit him! I didn't consider this extreme option for long. I'm five foot six, Malky is at least six foot three and 15 or 16 stone in weight. Those stats told me all I needed to know. It was not a battle I was likely to win. Instead we agreed that it was best for me to just ignore him. And I did. For four or five days I went into my shell, blanked him, didn't acknowledge his existence, didn't talk to him and treated him as though he were invisible.

To his great credit he took the initiative to take me to one side and ask what was going on. I had a go at him, telling him that he was out of order and over the top, and he apologised. He explained that he was just having a laugh and a joke. He didn't mean it and it wasn't personal. I've subsequently realised that it was his alpha male, macho way of showing that he liked me. That chat was such a relief for me and represented a turning point in our relationship. We've been big friends since. It was also a big learning point for me. I learned to address issues as they arose, rather than procrastinating, and I also learned that in football dressing rooms there will always be banter but not to take it to heart. It's certainly no place for the sensitive.

Almost every dressing room will be like that. It's part of the culture in football and you need to develop a ridiculously thick skin. It's almost an initiation that younger players have to go through. Particularly if you are innocent or gullible then you are bound to be on the receiving end of banter, wind-ups and practical jokes. In a strange way it is all part of your personal development, because when you play in front of a crowd they are not known for being sensitive to your feelings. You get dog's abuse sometimes, and if you are soft, weak or easily distressed then you will not be able to survive.

So, in some ways, the banter was part of my education, giving me a good grounding, hardening me up and providing me with valuable experience and coping strategies.

With hindsight I realise that the Norwich dressing room was probably a comparatively civil dressing room to be in. Matt Jackson, Craig Fleming, Malky MacKay – these were genuine, kind, good guys, who were the salt of the earth. It's not always like that. I've been in teams with malicious, horrible characters who enjoyed being cruel.

Thankfully I sorted things out with Malky, became more comfortable around my teammates, and became a fixture within the first 11. Now performing on a regular basis, I had to deal with the more typical challenges that every footballer faces: dealing with poor performances and the criticism that follows. Regardless of who you are, at times it will feel like the whole world is on your back.

The critics who I paid least attention to were the media. A lot of players say that they don't read the papers, but every coach that I've travelled on, both to and from a game, had the papers on board – broadsheets and tabloids – and the players read every word that was written about them. Why, I'm not too sure. My view is why would a professional footballer respect the views of someone who is only writing in the newspaper because they are good at English? They don't write because of their knowledge of football as none of them have played at any sort of level. So if it's just a journalist then why would you treat their opinion seriously and take it personally if they criticise you? Besides, they might not even have been at the game.

I also didn't pay much attention to the crowd. Sometimes, if you've been involved in an incident, the opposition fans might boo you. But I just took that as a compliment and it didn't bother me at all. Of course, it's probably a bit more challenging when your own supporters turn on you. I've seen players affected by that.

More generally I got much better with dealing with poor performances and setbacks after I did some work six or seven years ago with a psychology specialist called Keith Mincher. At the time he worked for Norwich City and has since progressed up to the England under-21s. He told me about a presupposition that 'there is no such thing as failure, only feedback'. Incidentally, once I had finished playing I completed my practitioner level of NLP (neuro-linguistic programming) and realised this is where Keith learned the concept. Those few words caused me to make a massive shift in my mindset. Up until then I didn't know that I didn't know how to deal with what I perceived as failure. As a result it was able to affect me. But with

Mincher's help I developed a strategy. Certainly it is a sentence worth pondering. If you are a striker and have a great chance to win the game but blaze it over the bar, Mincher is suggesting that you haven't necessarily failed – the feedback is that although you got into the right position you could have done better.

You may remember the famous Michael Jordan Nike advert where the most brilliant player ever to have set foot on a basketball court explains that during his career he missed 9000 shots, lost 300 games and missed 26 shots to win a game. He says that 'I missed over and over in my life, that's why I succeed'. Jordan's advice, of course, underlines the fact that a fear of falling short is not a reason to opt out or give up; in fact it's just a natural, healthy part of learning.

Consider the benefits of that approach. Feedback and failure are two very different emotions. If you don't see yourself as someone who failed – or worse still, as a failure – just someone who could have done better, that gives you a completely different mindset. You won't beat yourself up as much as I used to when I was younger. I think that many are like me and give themselves a hard time. In fact some don't even wait until they come off the pitch. I've seen so many players berating themselves during the game after they've messed up, constantly telling themselves how bad they are. You can never play well if you are thinking like that.

I think that you also need to be realistic and manage your own expectations. Football is a game of mistakes. The best players make less of them but everyone makes some. So if you are going to get down every time you make a mistake then you are going spend a lot of time with your chin on the ground. Perfection on a football pitch never happens unless your name is Lionel Messi.

As I matured I felt that the best way to deal with my own contribution, and whether we won or lost, was to keep on an even keel. If I played well and we won then I tried not to get too high; if I played badly and we lost then I tried not to get too low. That's just a professional mentality. Once one game is over, let it go and move on to the next – and when you get criticised respond on the pitch.

The only time I didn't feel able to do that was when I was playing in the senior Northern Ireland team and Lawrie Sanchez took over. He wanted to play the long ball, bypassing the midfield. I didn't suit the set-up of the team or the style of play, so I told him not to pick me. I suppose it was a sign of strength and my growing maturity that I felt assured enough to take that step.

By the time I left Norwich City at the end of the 2006/2007 season, in footballing terms I had been round the block a few times. I had played in the

Premier League, contested a Championship Play-Off final and had an extended taste of international football. And I had become smarter. Gradually I had learned and applied lessons in thinking that helped me to make the most of the God-given ability. I felt I had a resilience that had thickened, layer by layer, during my time as a professional. Little did I know when I packed my bags at Norwich City's Colney training ground and said my goodbyes to now former teammates that the next two years would examine that resilience to the full.

It was as though the fates had got together and conspired to test my spirit, self-motivation and positive attitude to breaking point with a series of challenges. If anything was going to wipe the smile off my face then 2007 and 2008 were most definitely the years. For much of that time I felt like a punch-drunk boxer. Each time I crawled up off the canvas another blow sent me down again.

When I left Norwich I headed to the Italian Alps and a two-week trial for Pisa. Playing in foreign football had always been desirable, not least because I knew my strong technical skills were ideally suited to that type of football. I trained well, won the bleep test and showed up strongly in the other physical challenges, played for 45 minutes in a trial game and scored. I couldn't have done more, but they failed to offer me a contract.

My next trial was at the Championship's Plymouth Argyle, managed by Ian Holloway. Over a frenetic fortnight of pre-season I scored seven goals in five games and got offered a six-month contract. Instead I opted for Luton Town of League One. Their offer was for two years and more money than Plymouth. My girlfriend was based in London and I decided that was the best choice. At first I thought I had landed on my feet. The club had a group of players and a manager in Kevin Blackwell that were capable of pushing for promotion – at least until two months into the season when the club plunged into administration. Ten points were deducted, and within a week two of our best players had been sold while those who remained didn't get paid. I could cope better than most. My career was well advanced and I had years of earning behind me, but some were not so fortunate. They had no savings and paying the mortgage proved impossible without the monthly pay packet. I must give credit to the manager, Kevin Blackwell, as he wrote out emergency cheques when he needed to until he got sacked in a cost-cutting exercise.

No one new could be brought in and it was little wonder that the survivors found it a challenge to stay motivated. In truth, many just gave up until a group bought the club. They brought in Mick Harford as manager, and after three months we started to be paid again. Yet it was too little, too late. Under the handicap of that 10-point deduction we were relegated into the depths of League Two. League One hadn't suited my game. There wasn't too much football being played. There was plenty of running but few passes, and the pitches were often poor. What would League Two feel like? It felt like the move to Luton had backfired.

That feeling was reinforced in the summer when the Football Association hit us with an absolute hammer blow. Due to further irregularities we were deducted 30 points. Thirty points! A deduction of this severity was unheard of. Even if we won our first 15 games we'd still be pretty much guaranteed to be bottom. Half of the boys thought 'what is the point of playing?' By Christmas that season we had played well but still hadn't erased the deduction.

This was mentally tough for all the players, and to keep upbeat and cheerful in these circumstances was beyond challenging. That was when I fell back most on the tools and techniques that I had learned. I chose to just treat each game in isolation and focus on winning it rather than dwelling on all the uncontrollable negatives surrounding the club's financial and league position. I chose to prepare and recover well from each game and stay professional. I chose not to act as one of the victims and to remain grateful for the opportunity to play professional football.

Funnily enough what helped me and the whole of the squad to keep going was the much-derided Johnson Paints Trophy. At least it gave us a potential moment of glory. I played in every game up to the final where we met Scunthorpe. Yet I was the only member of the squad who neither got picked for the starting 11 or the substitutes. I was absolutely gutted. We won, but it remains a bittersweet memory, another kick in the teeth.

Of course, in the league that 30-point deduction proved too much of a mountain to overcome and we were relegated to the Conference. Two seasons at Luton Town and two relegations, albeit both due to the penalties that we received for sins committed by previous administrations. It didn't feel good to have that on my CV, but at least I tried my best to stay upbeat throughout – helped immeasurably, I must say, by the fact that my personal life was stable and happy. I stayed with my fiancée in Harpenden, and having a solid foundation with family and friends was invaluable. It also gave me the impetus to try my luck in the United States to find a club after I left Luton.

Again I went to trial. I started with Darren Huckerby's team the San Jose Earthquakes, but they turned me down. Then I spent a week with Salt Lake City and they turned me down. Then I trialled for the Denver Colorado Rapids, where I excelled in every aspect of training. I've never had such a good week's training in my life. We were doing finishing sessions and every single time I was hitting the top corner. People were staying out to watch me. At the end of the trial I sat down expectantly with the manager Gary Smith. He said

'I can see why you've been an international and played in the Premier League. You've got great quality, you're brilliant with the lads, you boss the midfield, you understand the game, you communicate well, you've good speed and great technique.' His praise couldn't have been more fulsome, and I was lapping it up and expecting success – until he delivered the killer line: 'but I'm afraid you're not quite what we're looking for at the moment'. I couldn't believe it. I knew I had something to add to their team, and that rejection was difficult to take and a real challenge to my self-image. I didn't want my career to just peter out. It was a time when I really needed my mental skills to view this unfortunate series of events in a constructive way. Keith Mincher may have drummed it into me that there is no such thing as failure, just feedback, but I was getting a lot of feedback that wasn't putting a smile on my face.

Praise be, as ever, to Norwich City Football Club. They had been relegated into League One and Bryan Gunn was now in charge. Rather apologetically – considering I was already a member of the club's hall of fame – he said that I would need to go on trial again if I wanted to be considered. I swallowed my pride and this time it led to the offer of a contract. I was jubilant, partly because I was back at the club I loved, partly because my fiancée – Anna, who is a Norfolk girl – was working in the local hospital, and partly because I knew I had successfully endured all the knockbacks and been resilient enough to keep trying until I reached the outcome I wanted.

I had my medical on the same day as a certain Grant Holt, who had just joined from Shrewsbury Town, and I played my part in a promotion push under Paul Lambert that saw Norwich begin a meteoric rise back into England's Premier League. It also enabled me to end my career on a high and, to a large extent, on my own terms.

So, as we can see, my footballing life – like everyone else's – was a rollercoaster of highs and lows, with plenty of challenges and setbacks among the goals and the glory. Looking back, I think I got much better at dealing with adversity and, in particular, Keith Mincher's 'feedback not failure' concept really helped me and bolstered my mental state. At the risk of labouring the point, I found that one of the key benefits of dealing well with adversity was that it enabled me to maintain consistent levels of confidence and motivation. That in turn helped my performance. And with strong performances came better results.

Certainly, like most professional athletes I needed that confidence to play at the top of my game. It is clearly a critical quality yet it can be so elusive. When we've got it we're not quite sure how it got there and when it might leave us. And once it's gone, how can you get it back? Permanent self-confidence is the Holy Grail for any footballer, and by the end of my career

I came to the conclusion that to have any chance of achieving this I needed mental strength and a positive and helpful self-image.

I got better and better at this, but I was just an amateur compared to some of the master exponents that I played with. Over my career I can think of several players – with a wide range of different characters – whose confidence was pretty much bulletproof.

Craig Bellamy was one. After leaving Spurs and moving into the Championship with Norwich I thought I'd left behind those hugely confident people – and then I walked into the changing room and met Bellars!

You could see within 10 minutes that he had the exact same mentality and mindset as the top players. If you trained with him and did one bad pass he'd be on you, calling you names, telling you how rubbish you were. He just had such high standards and that's what I loved about him. As annoying as he was at times, I loved the fact that he had such high expectations for himself and others.

He came in as a 17-year-old into the first-team squad and hammered first-team players in their thirties. Some didn't like it – thinking 'who's this little shit thinking he can tell us what to do' – but others thought, 'no he's right'. He always thought that they shouldn't let their standards slip, that they should be raising their standards to his. That's why I respect Bellars, because he was always looking to improve.

Bellars is one of the few players that will talk his way through a football match, telling the defender how bad they are. He believes he's so much better than everyone else. Some defenders might think 'right, I'm going to get you', but because he's so quick and elusive they just wouldn't be able to.

He always comes off the pitch thinking he is the best player. Everyone else might disagree but he will still come off thinking he was the best. And because of that force field protecting his confidence Bellamy never hides and never plays it safe. In a crisis – when the going gets tough and the crowd are voicing their disapproval – some go missing or take the safe, sideways options when they receive the ball rather than attempting something difficult that might lead either to a goal-scoring opportunity or an interception.

Confidence was also never a problem for the fantastically talented Frenchman, David Ginola. He clearly had no issues with a poor self-image, low self-esteem or self-doubt. Quite the reverse. Like most of the elite performers, he really rated himself.

I remember when he was playing for Newcastle while I was in the youth team at Spurs – when he walked out of the dressing room at White Hart Lane everyone just turned and looked at him. He had the aura of a superstar about him. I was in awe of him, and it was a complete pleasure to watch him train because he oozed self-confidence and always expected to do well. Even when he was trying ridiculous shots from 35 yards he was disappointed if he didn't hit the target. He just had that overriding self-belief that everything he did was going to work out and a confidence that made him impervious to criticism. Indeed, his body language boasted 'I'm the best player on the pitch; give me the ball, because I'll do something with it.' If he tried to beat three or four players and they took the ball off him his teammates gave him a hard time, pleading with him to keep it simple – yet he was still saying 'no, give me the ball'. I really learned from Ginola. He had such a vast reservoir of self-esteem and self-assurance – and you couldn't really argue because he was such a phenomenal player.

My third and final example is Thierry Henry. He was another like Ginola – maybe it's a French trait – who had an aura. To sum him up I should just tell you about the experience I had playing against him. It was one of the first games of the season. Arsenal had just gone through the 2003/2004 season unbeaten as 'the Invincibles'. They hadn't lost all season, the first time anyone had done that.

It was so unfair because this guy was six foot three, the quickest player that's ever played in the Premiership, slowly dribbling towards me, teasing me, toying with me. His body language said 'don't come near me or I'm going to embarrass you'. My eyes closed and my heart sank, and I just kept backing off, backing off. The one time I tried to tackle him he eased into second gear and burned past me. I'm thinking 'where did he go?' and he was already 15 yards distant.

That just epitomised how much class, confidence, belief and style he had. For me he was the perfect footballer. If I could be reincarnated and come back playing football it would be in Henry's body. He had height, strength and pace. I remember the time he kicked a ball past Jamie Carragher, ran off the pitch, ran along the track at Anfield, got back on the pitch and still got to it ahead of an international defender. As if that wasn't enough he was, along with Alan Shearer, the best finisher the Premiership has seen. To combine all those attributes and abilities in one body should have been illegal. No wonder he was confident.

What did Bellamy, Ginola, Henry and – perhaps above all – Keith Mincher tell me about mental resilience? It seemed to be about creating a force field so that my confidence and self-esteem was impenetrable against the worst that could be thrown in my direction. Football is a game of mistakes. Shit happens. In the face of injuries, poor performance or the criticisms of others I needed to be unfazed, as bulletproof as possible, so that I could move on from the setback, look forward and think in a constructive way that helped me to play at my best in subsequent matches.

ROLE MODEL

Earlier in the chapter I talked about Craig Bellamy's strength, drive and confidence. He shares some common threads with Robert Green, now at Queens Park Rangers, as the player that most readily comes to mind when I think about mental resilience. They both developed an incredible, unbreakable self-belief, a determination to succeed and a tireless work ethic – and at one stage in their careers they were both often found in the gym at Norwich City's training ground at Colney. They weren't close friends and made a contrasting pair: Bellars was a complete loudmouth, always shouting off, while Greeny wouldn't say boo to a goose.

Robert Green: on England duty and as focused as ever. He is mentally strong and a tireless worker.

Goalkeepers need to be tougher than most because their blunders are so public and normally lead to a goal. Green makes a fascinating case study because he is not the stereotypical footballer. I first noticed that when I joined Norwich City, and he was 18 or 19 years of age and in the reserves. At that time he was still studying psychology at 'A' level because he knew the importance of getting educated. In normal day-to-day life it's not unusual for an 18-year-old to be taking a qualification, but it hardly ever happens in football, particularly when they already have a contract with a professional club. Certainly there was no one else studying at the time.

His work ethic also set him apart. He was always pushing himself, always the last to leave training; not by 30 minutes or an hour, but by two hours. He was sometimes there at 4.00 p.m. in the afternoon when everyone else had gone by 1.30 or 2.00. He had natural ability in abundance but at that stage he wasn't as athletic as he is now. So he worked on his size, strength and power, constantly training with the goalkeeping coach. He knew what he wanted, and nothing was going to stop him playing in the Premier League and representing his country.

What was most noticeable, though, was his relationship with the other players. In truth he never fully integrated with the team. He was quiet, polite and had a sense of humour, but he wasn't boisterous or involved in the laddish banter, jokes and chit-chat that went on in the dressing room. That was what I really liked about him. He wasn't a sheep and didn't feel the need to conform to football stereotypes. He was clearly mentally tough, because he just didn't care. He was his own person and knew exactly what he wanted to do. Even then you could see how driven he was and how much he wanted to achieve. His whole demeanour said 'I'm here to play football, I'm here to improve'.

As a result of this he was not particularly popular in the changing room. A lot of players didn't really get on with him as much as they could have done. They didn't see him as a typical footballer, didn't understand him. But that was all about their ignorance and their problem, not his. So he became a young man apart. Part of that was down to his innate character. In addition I think he was, perhaps subconsciously, already adopting some of the psychological techniques that I've outlined in this book. Certainly I was happy to watch him and learn; not least because I didn't fit the football stereotypes either.

Of course, Robert Green's mental resilience was tested to breaking point over the coming years. All goalkeepers suffer their share of calamities and it's how they deal with them that makes the difference. He had one mishap when he had just made it into the first team. Against Derby County he tried to hack a 30-yard back pass up the field – it took a horrible bounce and bobbled up over his foot and into the net. It was embarrassing and we lost the game as a result.

Yet he'd already dealt with it by the time he came into the dressing room afterwards. He wasn't beating himself up. He said 'I tried to clear it, I tried to do the right thing and you can't legislate for it bobbling up over my foot'. For me that was a real sign that he knew how to deal with setbacks. He was not deterred by criticism from his own players or the fans. He would still go out and perform every week, establishing himself as one of the finest goalkeepers in the country. He was outstanding for Norwich before moving to West Ham on a four-year deal where he was also excellent, progressing into the England squad and then the England team.

Having made his debut against Colombia he was selected for the 2006 World Cup squad. However, he seriously ruptured his groin while taking a goal kick during the England B international against Belarus and missed not only the finals but also the start of the next domestic season.

During his recovery from this long-term injury he had to deal with a challenge that I generally managed to dodge. Unless you work in football people don't understand that if you're injured you literally get cast aside. It's amazing. You can be your team's Wayne Rooney – the main man, the number one player, first on the team sheet – and then you get injured and no one cares about you. You're not involved in the training or the matches, you don't have any dealings with the manager and you are left on your own programme, working with the physio from 9.00 a.m. in the morning to 5.00 p.m. in the evening, trying to rehabilitate.

That can be mentally draining for footballers. They are used to being in a group, laughing and joking, enjoying the banter, but when you're injured a lot of players feel worthless. So your whole focus needs to be channelled towards doing everything that the physio asks of you. You might be asked to take your ice packs and equipment home to do some rehab, but some players just leave them at the door. What's needed is full commitment to getting back as quickly as you can.

When it comes to the healing process it isn't just the body that needs to be repaired, it's the mind. I've known people who have come back from knee and ankle injuries and they've felt that it just isn't right even though physically it is healed. Psychologically they are worried about putting pressure on it or going 100 per cent into a tackle. That's where visualisation can help – imagining being back in the fray and committing to 50–50 challenges. But Robert Green recovered to get back into the England squad, and four years after missing out on Germany in 2006 he was selected for the 2010 World Cup Finals in South Africa.

Little did he know that his force field of strength and confidence would face the acid test after he was selected for the opening match against United States. England took an early lead – then, in the 40th minute, Clint Dempsey tried a tame, long-range effort. It was the kind of shot that Green had successfully saved a million times in the past yet, inexplicably, he let it slip past him, dribbling into the net. The match finished in a draw and, on the biggest stage in world football, he had clearly been culpable. He incurred the ridicule of the media and the wrath of the whole country. Manager Fabio Capello replaced him with David James in subsequent games and he was omitted from the first England squad named after the tournament for a friendly against Hungary.

Many, perhaps most, would not have recovered from such a high-profile error. However, back at West Ham he continued to use the psychological techniques that had helped him to make it into the England team to begin with, decided that this one mistake wasn't going to ruin his career, and gradually began to turn in outstanding performances again. He was back to being a top, top keeper and was rewarded by being brought back into the squad for the Euro 2012 qualifier against Montenegro in October 2010. To be able to deal with what happened in the World Cup and come back as well as he did the next season shows just how exceptionally durable he is.

KEY MESSAGES

There is no such thing as failure, just feedback. High performers don't view 'failure' in the same way as lower performers. They just see it as a bump along the road and it doesn't impact their confidence in any way.

Mental strength, self-belief and a positive self-image are attributes that will help us to thrive under challenges and when things don't work out as intended.

If we become skilled at dealing with adversity then it helps us to build a bulletproof, robust confidence – a trait that is essential to consistently achieving peak performances.

LESSON SEVEN

MIX INTENSITY WITH CONTROL

The worst example I have seen of intensity without control is Joey Barton. He clearly has ability and has played a lot of his career in the Premier League, but if I were a manager I'd never have him in my team because, in my opinion, his attitude and mindset is so bad. I could give numerous examples when he has been out of control both on and off the pitch. The most obvious example was for Queens Park Rangers playing against Manchester City on the last day of the 2011/2012 season. The title was up for grabs for City and if results went against QPR they could have gone down. Barton was captain and supposed to be leading by example, but as the game reached its critical moments he got into a fracas with three or four Manchester City players and was sent off. QPR and Barton got lucky. With a different set of results his petulance could have cost up to £90 million, just for the sake of getting one over on someone.

Barton is at one end of the spectrum and, in my opinion, is deficient in this area. Not far away is the Italian Mario Balotelli, who could keep a sports psychologist occupied 24/7 trying to work out what's going on inside his head. I'm not sure even he knows, and therefore he is a fascinating subject for analysis.

In some ways he has a lot going for him. He has such natural gifts. He has great coordination and ball sense, is balanced, can control a ball, is two-footed and scores goals so easily. He also has all the required physical attributes: six foot two tall, quick and powerful. And he doesn't appear to feel pressure. I remember watching him score a critical, late penalty in a televised game against Tottenham. He just stroked it into the corner with consummate ease as if he was on the training ground. After the game the interviewer asked him about how he coped with the pressure – and it was clear that the whole concept was alien to him. Pressure? What pressure? He just didn't feel any. He has got such self-belief and confidence – some might label it ego or arrogance – that the thought of missing did not even enter his mind. That, of course, helped him to score because all of his focus was pointing towards success. So there is much in his mental make-up to admire: a strong self-image, a force field of confidence and the ability to channel his thinking positively.

Yet for all those riches, in my opinion he currently has psychological flaws. Indeed, I think that his lack of control and erratic nature – bearing in mind that at the time of writing he is 22 years old and no longer a fledgling footballer – may ultimately prevent him from enjoying the long-term professional career that he is capable of.

Balotelli should be one of the first names on the team sheet for club and country. Yet that's not the case. When things go badly – someone kicks him, a refereeing decision goes against him – then he can be a liability. He also appears to lack control off the pitch, which suggests that he doesn't take personal responsibility for his own actions. I'd love to spend 30 minutes with him to see if I could get inside his head. But many managers have already tried that and come up short. The training ground bust-up with Roberto Mancini highlighted the size of the challenge. It remains to be seen if Balotelli changes his ways at AC Milan, but the early signs were not promising. He seems to bring the circus with him wherever he goes. He remains a hard to handle yet fascinating character and a firecracker of a footballer. If my analysis of the modern game is accurate then Balotelli will need to address his own psychology if he is to sustain a long-term career at the highest level. It will be fascinating to see if he can manage it and no doubt the support staff at AC Milan are working with him to that end. The stupid footballer may be dead, but Mario Balotelli is far from stupid and he has the capability to achieve great things.

Maybe Balotelli should take note from another who has had issues with control. Wayne Rooney is a world-class footballer, one of my favourites. His achievements are immense; he has so much class and ability, and I love watching him play. But I have to say that there have been times in the past when, like Balotelli, he has also been petulant and immature.

He was certainly petulant and immature when, in the 2006 World Cup quarter-final, he stamped on Portugal's defender Ricardo Carvalho in front of the referee and was promptly sent off. Although the game was locked in a 0–0 stalemate, England were gaining the ascendancy. This was the best chance of glory for their so-called golden generation – Neville, Cole, Beckham, Terry, Ferdinand, Gerrard, Lampard and the like – and Rooney's unthinking assault probably cost them the game, which they ultimately lost on penalties, and the chance of winning a major international tournament.

He was also petulant and immature in the 74th minute of the crucial European Championship qualifying game in Macedonia in October 2011 when, for no great reason, he kicked out at a defender and received another straight red card. Although England hung on, just, to confirm their qualification for the finals, Rooney missed the early stages because of his resulting suspension.

I suppose some would put Rooney's sending off against Portugal down to inexperience – the impetuosity of youth. At that stage he was only 20 years old. However, he was nearly 26 at the time of the Macedonia red card and there wasn't much evidence that he had learned a lot during that intervening period.

For me, Rooney has been an enigma. I think he is slowly maturing and he does appear to be learning from his mistakes, which is just as well because the definition of insanity is to keep doing the same things over and over and expecting a different result. There are promising signs that he is getting into fewer disciplinary problems and missing out on fewer big games. That's good because it's certainly been a problem, not just for his own career and what he will ultimately achieve in the game but in the way that he penalised either his country or his club. There's simply too much at stake to keep making these errors when they are within his control. He's one of the biggest earners in football, and with a fat pay packet comes responsibilities. Top players are paid top rates, and if they dive into a hot-headed challenge and get suspended it is the team that suffers, in vast amounts of wasted wages as well as the absence of one of their most influential players.

I certainly don't agree with those who used say that you have to accept talented but hot-headed footballers like Barton, Balotelli and Rooney (at least the younger version) as they are; that if you take away their edge then they'll be half the player. That's rubbish. There is absolutely no relationship between reacting aggressively to an incident and striking a shot into the top corner. If those unpleasant streaks were removed from their games they'd still be left with the same hunger and desire to win. Everyone who plays professional football is competitive and forceful, but few act in the way that these players have done at times. Personally I don't blame anyone other than the player. It's their problem and they need to break the habit.

I guess the starting point to finding a solution is to understand the causes. It is no coincidence that most incidents happen in games where the stakes are high. That gives us some obvious clues, because it is clear that being able to cope with challenging circumstances, environments and situations is essential to keeping things under control. Without self-control some players move out of their normal emotional state, both before the match and sometimes during it – and where there is intensity without self-control then players can erupt and suffer the consequences.

I suspect that part of the problem is getting too pumped up and too 'psyched'. Remember my hero Paul Gascoigne in the 1991 FA Cup final against Nottingham Forest? Eyes bulging, he charged around mindlessly, not in control of his emotions, too pumped for his own good. If he hadn't injured himself so badly with a rash tackle he would surely have been sent off. He was way above the emotional zone he needed to be in to play well.

In addition to big-match occasions, refereeing decisions and the actions of opponents can cause the red mist to descend. The ex-Arsenal and England striker Ian Wright was one who aimed to wind up and provoke. He talked all the way through each game and gave every defender he played against an earbashing, telling them how terrible they were and that they shouldn't be on the same pitch. Craig Bellamy is the same, constantly at his opponents, telling them they should be doing his gardening!

I remember playing against Kevin Muscat of Wolves. I'd heard about his reputation, and how he'd tackled Craig Bellamy and torn his cruciate ligaments. Teammates warned me that he'd look to get inside my head and wind me up. After about 30 minutes of the match the stream of abuse started – he told me that I was Irish and small which, to be honest, I was already aware of. It was all the normal stuff. I let my feet do the talking, kept running at him with the ball, dribbling past him and eventually he became less worried about me and more about his defending.

I never bothered about players like Muscat. There's always a lot of talk on the pitch, someone saying something to wind you up, giving you a hard time verbally, looking for a reaction. I just thought it was all sticks and stones. They're not actually causing you pain; they're just words. If you are petulant, immature or inexperienced enough not to handle something like that then so be it – but I was unfazed, and equally, I never gave stick out because I didn't feel it would help my game.

Of course there is a line that even in professional sport you wouldn't expect an opponent to cross. Zinedine Zidane clearly felt that line had been crossed by the words of the Italian defender Marco Materazzi in the 2006 World Cup Final. There were just 10 minutes to go in the match – indeed, in Zidane's illustrious career – when he was sensationally sent off after headbutting Materazzi in the chest.

Since then there has been a lot of conjecture over what was said to Zidane, but clearly whatever it was caused such an extreme reaction that he would have taken affront regardless of whether he was at work, down the pub or on a football pitch playing the critical last moments in a World Cup Final in front of an audience of billions.

Zidane's view was 'I don't care where I am and who's watching, if someone says that to me then I'm going to react'. In fact four years after the incident he said that he 'would rather die' than apologise to Materazzi and added that he 'could never have lived with himself' had he been allowed to remain on the pitch and help France win the match.

I do have some sympathy for Zidane, and clearly he had been targeted by an opponent and deliberately provoked beyond his breaking point at that precise moment. But generally the provocation in football does not demand such an extreme reaction. You may get a tackle across the shins or be tripped up when you are running, but just compare it to rugby, where someone could stand on your neck, gouge your eye or punch your face. Provocation there is at a completely different level – and yet most of the time those players don't react because they've got such discipline, have been trained in such a way, and there is a culture in rugby that means you don't react no matter what happens and you let the referee deal with it.

My Zidane–Materazzi equivalent could have happened at the New Den, playing against Millwall in 2003. I kept having tussles and tackles with their midfielder, Tim Cahill, and about halfway through the game there was another tough challenge. Both of us got up and he jogged past me and spat in my face. For me, if someone does that they are the lowest of the low. It would have been very easy for the red mist to have descended and I think most people would have understood if I had punched Cahill in the face. But I didn't. I responded in a way that was going to allow me to stay on the pitch, and I just tried to get my own back on him in a challenge. I didn't spit in his face because I had more dignity and higher standards than to drop to his level and follow what he had done to me.

My dad. My role model and a hugely positive influence throughout my life.

That said, I'm no angel. My dad, who has had such a positive influence on my career, used to follow me when I was playing as a youngster, and if I was ever on the end of rough treatment he used to stand on the side of the pitch and clench his fist to me. He wasn't suggesting that I should punch the opponent or that he would punch me. The message was to get stuck in – and because of my size, it was doubly important for me to stick up for myself and be aggressive on the pitch.

Generally I was able to keep my aggression under control. However, I did get sent off playing for Norwich against Cardiff. I was tackled at thigh level, and that time I reacted rather than responded. I pushed my head towards the defender and that was viewed by the referee as warranting a red card. Interestingly, that game was my first under a new manager at Carrow Road and I wasn't a regular in the side. Peter Grant had just taken over, and when I came on as a second-half substitute I was keen to impress, perhaps too psyched up. That led me to lose control, whereas at the time of the Cahill spitting incident I was playing regularly and recognised as a key cog within the team. So perhaps my emotional state was more stable.

Certainly there are plenty of potential trigger points that can cause an emotional imbalance, an impulsive moment of madness that you later regret. But how can a footballer condition himself to stay calm and in control? How can he avoid letting his club or country down by getting sent off in a big game?

Without doubt the aim is to respond rather than react, to be in control of every action we take. How can we do that? I think that the likes of Balotelli need to work at it, probably with a mental coach. He needs to put himself into these flashpoint situations in training or spend some time visualising someone coming through the back of him or taking him around the knees. He needs to see himself taking a breath, dusting himself down, getting up and letting the referee deal with it. And if he does that over and over and over again then it will become so much a part of his subconscious that he might react differently the next time it happens in a key match.

Above all, Balotelli, and other footballers, need to take responsibility for their thinking and the way they deal with what most would perceive as high-pressure matches and pressurised moments during a match. I write 'perceive' because I want to throw it out there that there is no such thing as pressure.

I know that's a massive statement that most people will disagree with. Managers talk about it, reporters talk about it, journalists talk about it. Yet pressure isn't something that you can grab hold of. It's not tangible. You can't measure it. It's not a thing, a place, a destination. It doesn't just arrive at a stadium on match day. When players go into games pressure only exists in their heads. It's just a tag that they apply to an emotion that they have created. Consequently, for me, there's no such thing as pressure.

Before most games I was aware of changes in my physical state. I got butterflies in the pit of my stomach, my heartbeat raced and on two occasions that come to mind – my debut for Tottenham and the Championship Play-Off final with Norwich – my mouth was still dry 20 minutes into the game. I noticed that teammates also displayed other changes: some were in the toilet every five minutes leading up to kick off, some went quiet, some got loud, some developed a bit of a shake and there were some who were physically sick.

Were these changes good or bad, helpful or unhelpful? I think the answer to that question is entirely down to the label that was applied by each player in his own head. If the player associated the feelings with negative emotions such as fear, dread and anxiety then it wouldn't have helped them play well, but if they associated the feelings with excitement and anticipation then it would have probably helped them. I am certain that it's possible to talk your way in or out of a performance.

Perhaps that's why some thrive and some wilt on the big occasion. Perhaps it's back to mental resilience and your personal force field. Real Madrid's Cristiano Ronaldo has that confidence that means he just doesn't feel pressure. He wants to play on the biggest stage, in front of the biggest crowds. And I remember Dion Dublin telling me about the day Eric Cantona joined Manchester United from Leeds. At that stage he wasn't the legend he is now. But apparently from day one Cantona's whole demeanour and language told everyone that this was where he belonged and where he deserved to be. He loved being in the spotlight and relished the big occasion, seeing it as an opportunity to showcase his talent.

The likes of Ronaldo and Cantona know that their talent is innate, is part of them and that they can rely on it. They do not doubt whether they will perform well, they simply speculate how well they will perform, boosted by tapping into the positive memories of playing well in the past. They know that they would only be stifled if they suffered from nerves and tension.

Yet, at the other end of the spectrum, there are those who freeze on the big stage, in front of big crowds. Of course, you just can't play professional football unless you can cope with performing in front of a crowd. Those who struggle with that don't get too far because they go back to being amateurs when it comes to performing under pressure.

It's ironic really, because you need the fans there to create an atmosphere – playing in an empty stadium is soul-destroying – but at the same time you need to be able to block them out and concentrate on the job in hand. Some learn to do that, others don't. They struggle to control their nerves and they tend to fall by the wayside.

I mentioned that I used to play with seasoned professionals who were sick in the toilets before games. I could never understand that. This was all happening in their heads. They were clearly building it up so much and were emotionally caught up in the situation. It's not like it happened anywhere else. They didn't go down to the shops and throw up on the way. That kind of extreme physical response to anxiety was driven by doubts about whether they could deal with the challenge ahead. Sometimes that feeling can translate into freezing on the pitch, and sometimes it's not just individuals but the whole team. When Norwich lost at Fulham by six goals on the last day of the 2004/2005 season – needing a win to stay in the Premier League – we froze. Similarly when Ipswich lost by a record 9–0 at Anfield against Liverpool. Scores like that don't happen unless the team freezes.

So I worked to try to ensure that I viewed what we'll call 'butterflies' in a positive and constructive light, helping them to work for me instead of against me. That gave me the best chance of getting into that ideal emotional state when I crossed the white line just before kick off so I had both intensity *and* control.

Funnily enough, it's when there were no signs from my body before a game that I found I should worry. Just as it is possible to be overhyped and too psyched up, it is entirely possible to feel flat and lacklustre. The thought of playing a game of professional football in front of a large crowd would be viewed by many as an amazing dream. Yet when it becomes the norm sometimes it can feel like Groundhog Day, and there have been times when I have gone through the motions. I think it's just human nature, even for the elite performers playing for the top clubs in the Premier League.

They may have one of the most envied jobs in the world – getting paid mind-blowing amounts of money per week; being famous and admired, and showing off their ample skills twice a week in front of 70,000 adoring fans at the ground and billions all around the world. Yet it is not possible to remain on a motivational high the whole time. Adrenalin has to have peaks and troughs, and eventually that pattern becomes their version of *normal*. At worst it can become mundane. Even at my level, I went through spells in my career where I stopped getting the same buzz from playing, and it felt more like a job than a privilege. When that is the case it can be difficult to keep building yourself for each new challenge.

Yet a footballer who plays without intensity is not going to last long. That's why I so admire that small and elite group – the Lampards, the Gerrards, the Giggses – who can sustain an elevated level of motivation and performance for 60 games a season over 12 or 13 years. That really is a mind-blowing emotional and physical achievement.

In summary, I'd say that I learned that the key for me was to copy the elite and go into games motivated, alert and excited, but not too anxious or hyper. I got better at achieving that as I adopted a consistent and regimented preparation before a game (see Lesson Ten, page 109), and I think I was helped by a natural inclination to place the match in proper perspective. I always knew it was just a game, no matter how well I wanted to perform and no matter how keen I was to end it on the winning side.

ROLE MODEL

I found role models easy to define for this chapter. Straight away a player and an international team came into mind. If we start with the player first – Scott Parker is a perfect role model. Off the pitch he is humble, a family man, soft-spoken and quiet. On the pitch, however, he gives everything in every game he plays. He is so committed, so full-blooded, and flies into tackles – some of which he wins just through sheer desire and passion.

Scott Parker: the epitome of intensity with control.

Earlier in his career he came on loan to Norwich City from Charlton Athletic and I was immediately aware that he was a player with great potential. He was just so obviously a winner. He certainly had the intensity, and some of his challenges – even in training – made me wince. But as he has matured he has retained this intensity while ensuring that he always has full emotional control. So even after the most full-blooded challenges he just gets up and walks away. There is no testosterone-driven desire to pick a fight, no petulance. He plays with both his heart and his head, and I liken that approach to the best rugby players. Rugby is a game of extreme physical contact but the players generally manage to keep a cool head and their emotions in check.

Managers certainly love Parker's approach. I remember Harry Redknapp saying that he wished he had a squad with Parker's attitude, and it has earned him international recognition. He was England's Player of the Year in 2011, and named England captain against Holland in February 2012.

By the way, one of the other aspects I admire about Parker is that he quite openly admits to working with a psychologist, Mike Griffiths. In 2011 Parker said in an article in the *Daily Mail* by Matt Lawton:

It was probably two years ago that Mike came into my life and into my career. To find your weaknesses on the field can be quite easy. If you're weak on your left foot you go and hit some more balls.

But for a footballer to admit there might be a mental weakness there, that maybe at times their thoughts decapitate them, that they can't perform at the level they want to, is not easy. It's not something players like to admit to, because it does sound like a weakness. Nobody wants to admit that they've panicked because there are 60,000 people out there and they can't perform.

But I realised I was the sort of person who would think a lot and probably analyse things too much. And at times I felt it was holding me back, and I knew if I could improve that part of my game it would help me.

Mike has helped me no end. Speaking to him, him understanding me, using different techniques. We speak religiously the day before a game. It's helped massively.

He puts things into perspective for me, because it is just a football match. We are all human. We all feel the same things. I get paid to play football but I'm also a normal bloke and if I give the ball away three times on the bounce I'm going to start thinking, 'Bloody hell, it's going to be one of those days'. And it's those kinds of thoughts that can paralyse a player.

So Parker has been clever enough to tap into the expertise around him, and that will have undoubtedly helped him to be able to play at full-on intensity without losing his cool, traits that are very much in synch with the international team that came into my mind.

German efficiency is a stereotype, a cliché that has a lot of truth in it. I really admire the way Germany play. They have intensity and passion in their football, but ice in their blood. They are cool and calculating, and ruthlessly effective in what they do. I'm tempted to say that they have taken the emotion out of playing, but that's not true. It is definitely there but camouflaged under this utter professionalism and overwhelming desire to just get on with their jobs and win.

There are no egos in their team. The current side contains some amazing talent – Mesut Özil, Bastian Schweinsteiger, Philipp Lahm, Thomas Müller – but all of them put the team above self. They are just so well drilled and oiled, and the strength of their mentality means they do not unravel under stress. I commend the German mentality, and if we were creating the perfect young player I would merge that brainpower with the technical ability of the Spanish.

KEY MESSAGES

In football – and many other walks of life – it is important and possible to mix passion and control.

When we are in this optimum state it allows us to make rational and helpful decisions but remain highly motivated with a drive and hunger to succeed.

Pressure is not tangible and only exists in our minds. External events cannot create pressure unless we allow them to. That's why different people feel pressure in different ways and at different times.

LESSON EIGHT

INNOVATE, ANALYSE, IMPROVE

The speed of modern football is remarkable in many ways. The speed of the action on the pitch; speed in the development of new approaches to match-day preparation and recovery; speed in the turnover of managers, support staff and teammates that a professional footballer works with. Change happens at a dizzying speed and the only constant in modern-day football is that there will always be change.

So it's no place for the stick-in-the-mud. Those who stand still stagnate and get left behind. The game moves on without them. No doubt the skill sets required of a professional footballer in the modern game have developed since I started out – and I am certain that the skill sets required of 2020's footballers will have evolved still further.

The stupid footballers will only be comfortable doing what they've always done. They will be blinkered and resistant to what they see as unnecessary upheaval and, as a result, become sporting dinosaurs. The minimum requirement is to be aware of and keep abreast of new trends. But that's only just enough not to go backwards. The smart ones are the visionaries who look to the future, embrace the change and get ahead of the game.

Of course the football clubs usually lead the way, and advances in sports science are moving at a great speed. Once, ice baths and computerised analysis of opponents were new and cutting-edge ideas. Now everyone is doing it.

Each season more progress is made. At the time of writing new trends include:

- Fitting players with heart-rate monitors and GPS trackers that enable researchers to provide an immediate breakdown of their performance stats after training.
- Vitamin D beds – similar to a walk-in sunbed without the damaging rays.
- Gravity-free or underwater treadmills.

But by the time these words are read things will have moved on again. These innovations are all in the name of getting an edge over the opposition, and clubs will go to great lengths and immense costs to do so.

The same mindset is freely available to each footballer, and certainly, in an era when football was less keen to embrace it, innovative thinking was an underlying theme throughout my sporting life. As I matured through my teenage years I researched and tried out different ways to help me make the most of my God-given talent. Nearly 50 years ago, the England manager Sir Alf Ramsey said that one of his international players, Martin Peters, was 'ten years ahead of his time'. I couldn't claim to be that on the pitch, but in terms of my approach I look back and realise that I was embracing certain helpful habits 10 years before they became widely adopted. I think that was partly driven by my desire to improve and also my inquisitive nature. I always wanted to know why and always questioned things – and I eventually undertook a sports science degree at Manchester University so that I knew the theory as well as the practice.

In other chapters I've written about my approach to goal setting and visualisation (see Lesson Three, page 35). In addition, when I was about 18 my mum started telling me about the benefits of yoga. At first I was dismissive. I thought yoga was a social pastime for middle-aged women at the village hall, but eventually I considered the potential gains: greater flexibility, stronger core muscles, and improved balance. Every single gain would clearly be an attribute for the physical side of football and help me in my desire to leave football injury-free. So I bought a video (for any youngsters reading this, ask your parents what one of those are) and tried it.

At that stage a footballer who admitted he was doing yoga would have been seen as big girl's blouse and been on the receiving end of some unmerciful stick in the dressing room, so I restricted the sessions to my house. I got up earlier, did a yoga session, and went into training having already stretched. I soon felt the benefits.

Yoga stretches the muscles for longer, and modern research has shown that this is far better for you than the short, static stretches that tend to be done on the training ground. I did yoga virtually every other day for 17 years in football, and I'm still doing it now that it's become trendy and commonplace to build up core muscle groups. Ryan Giggs took up yoga late in his illustrious career (in his mid-thirties), and is now an advocate – but I was doing that 15 years ago. It's no coincidence that I suffered virtually no muscle injuries during my career.

Another area is supplements, which are a good example of how the game has changed. In athletics, supplements are widely used to replenish muscle stores and aid recovery from physical exertion. The World Health Organization recommends five portions of fruit and vegetables a day. That's for someone who sits in an office, so how much does a footballer who is doing two to three hours of physical training need? Probably 15 to 20. It is very difficult to consume that much, and supplements are a fast and easy way to get your dietary requirements in one hit. So supplements are widely available in football clubs. Everyone should know the benefits, but many just don't get round to taking them. They procrastinate, they forget. It's just not good enough if you want to make the most of your ability. As supplements came into the game I always made sure I made full use of the opportunity.

So I was innovative on the physical side of the game and also forward-thinking on the mental side, an area where football is still way behind other sports. From the age of 18 I used to get on a train every week for two to three years to travel to Roehampton and see a sports psychologist called Dr Craig Mahoney to talk about my mindset and improve my thinking habits. Again, I saw the value but, again, I kept it to myself because both the players and the management would have misunderstood me. It would have been seen as a sign of weakness, whereas it was building upon strength.

I was also a bit different when it came to the post-match analysis of my performance. As my career progressed I felt that I needed an objective view of how I'd performed. I remember our coach, Keith Mincher, telling me that I needed to have a strong understanding of my 'clear and current reality'. He didn't ask 'how are you?', he asked 'where are you at?' His view was that only if you had an awareness of where 'you're at' could you know what to work on and improve.

Certainly the more traditional ways of getting feedback on my performance just didn't do it for me. For instance, the moments after a game has finished are not moments of cold, sober reflection for fans, players or managers alike. Emotions can run high and opinions can be clouded. The manager, for instance, might have laid into me for not taking a chance or not working hard enough, but his views were likely to be unduly influenced by extreme emotions in the heat of the moment. They didn't take into account the whole of the 90 minutes, and his opinions might have been influenced by what he already thought about me. So I never put much store by this instant post-match reaction of the manager or, indeed, myself.

In the early days my post-match mood would be unduly influenced by whether I'd missed a sitter or scored a screamer, whether we'd won or lost. Those emotions stayed with me for quite a long time and were pretty unhelpful. I could act like a bear with a sore head through to the beginning of the next week, beating myself up for no great benefit and based on just a few key moments rather than on my overall contribution. How conducive is that for elite performance?

As I matured and reached my mid-twenties I began to analyse my performance in different, more objective ways. On a Monday I used to be given a DVD of the game provided by our sports scientist, Dave Carolan. It provided all the footage and information needed, and I'd go home and work through the DVD. It helped me to see things that I wasn't aware of during the game, when I might be caught up in what I was doing and be unaware of what was happening on the other side of the pitch.

Additionally, I created a homemade scoring system of how I'd performed. I gave myself a mark depending on my contribution – for example, if I scored a goal, provided an assist, crossed to create a chance, passed or tracked back. All these different facets allowed me to dissect and measure my performance in a more scientific way.

Nowadays there are much more sophisticated options to measure performance, but I was just trying to give myself a benchmark each week so I could understand and self-analyse rather than read in a newspaper that I got a six out of ten from a guy who might not have been at the game! It certainly helped me to introspectively analyse my game and define what I was doing well and what I wasn't doing well. That was critical to help me pinpoint my strengths and weaknesses, and then work on them.

If those statistics showed that I attempted 10 passes with my left foot in a game and I gave away eight of them, alarm bells would go off, highlighting that although I might subjectively believe my left foot is ok, I keep giving the ball away and so that's something I should work on. I'd then focus on that during training.

An even better example of this was my left-foot crossing. Although I was a right-footer I played most of my career on the left side. Generally I looked to cut in on my right foot and have a shot on goal, but often the defender would force me down the line onto my left foot. When I did go down the line sometimes the cross wasn't accurate or failed to create opportunities for the strikers. That became a key development area. I vowed to turn the weakness into a strength – so I set goals for it, worked hard two or three times a week in training, and improved to the level where, four or five years later at the age of 27 or 28, I was so confident that I'd take corners left-footed, and my general play and crossing on my left foot was almost as good as on my right. Of course my analysis of games enabled me to measure my improvement.

I also began to rate myself in the kind of areas I've focused on in this book: how I saw myself in terms of confidence or communication, or dealing with criticism. I also analysed upcoming opponents. Going into a game the team would review videos so that we could better understand how they played tactically, likely set plays, their key players and so on. The majority of the information came from the manager and coaches, but if I were playing against someone who promised to be a particularly challenging opponent then I'd ask for further information or footage, or maybe even phone up players in other teams.

Overall, I think that this kind of analysis and innovation was a key part of me becoming a good professional, particularly because it was allied to goal setting and a desire to put in hard graft to get better. There really is no other way. All the footballers who have made it to the top are eager to learn and have a strong work ethic. They wouldn't have got far without it, and I felt self-motivated to improve my own game regardless of whether there was pressure on me from others.

It certainly wasn't the manager telling me to stay behind after training; I was the one doing that. He wasn't telling me to use visualisation to supplement my work on the training ground. Yet before getting up in the morning I chose to stay in bed for an extra 15–20 minutes to visualise a skill – crossing with my left or cutting in and curling a right-foot shot into the top right-hand corner – that would improve my game. I'd picture it, creating and strengthening my own neural pathways in my head, and then used that muscle memory to practise it at match tempo during and after training.

When a proactive attitude towards innovation is paired with a drive to work hard then it's almost inevitable that the results will follow. It's no coincidence that the elite performers in most sports are also the obsessives who shed more sweat than everyone else. It's not just those who want to reach the top, but those who are already at the summit yet keep on pushing themselves when lesser mortals would have long relaxed. Sometimes it's good to think about other sports in this context, as well as football – and three sportsmen come into to my mind whose dedication to excellence has gone above and beyond what anyone could have reasonably expected of them.

The first one is Michael Jordan, who became probably the best basketball player ever and yet constantly wanted to improve. He never dropped his standards down to the players he was playing against. The way he kept improving was to be aware of his weaknesses and then transform them into his strengths.

Then I think of rugby union's Jonny Wilkinson. Wilkinson was one of the best rugby players and sportsmen in the world, and he took discipline and professionalism to a new level. I remember watching him on a television programme and he was doing circuit training involving chin-ups, squats and the like. Normally footballers do a minute on and a minute off for 20 minutes, but he was doing every exercise in the circuit with no break at all for 45 minutes. I had never seen anyone able to do that much and exhibit such power, strength and fitness.

He was just as disciplined on the training ground as in the gym. I remember him talking about how he used to practise kicking field goals until it got so dark that he couldn't see the posts. That was just incredible dedication, professionalism and, perhaps, a touch of mania. One of the reasons why he gained such a glittering reputation in world rugby is that he was on the training ground so long after everyone else had gone home.

Third, I think of my own sport and David Beckham. I have so much admiration for him because he has such an abundance of everything – league titles, money, cars, fame – but he is still so professional and dedicated in everything he does. One of the reasons why he's been one of the best free-kick takers in the world is because he constantly practises, searching for that perfection.

These are great examples for any footballer at any level, because they are athletes who have clearly said to themselves 'this is what it takes to be the best, I'm prepared to do it', and then they've gone and made it happen. Interestingly, sports psychologists are reported as saying that Premier League footballers are among the most difficult sports performers to motivate because they are so rich and pampered – they become lax, complacent and resistant to guidance. As one exasperated manager said: 'how do you make a millionaire sweat?'

Well, the bank balances of Jordan, Wilkinson and Beckham are presumably healthy enough. Yet it hasn't diminished their hunger. Why do they do it? What keeps driving them on? I'm not sure they will really know. It's just something deep within them – definitely a love of their sport, of winning and the thrill of competition, and definitely an unyielding commitment to high standards. Perhaps there is also a fear of failure. It's just part of our make-up that people will do more to avoid pain than they will to gain pleasure. One thing is for certain: I found that the unrelenting will to keep finding an edge is one of the healthiest possible traits you can have, both in sport and beyond.

ROLE MODEL

I played against Cristiano Ronaldo during his first season at Manchester United. In fact we both came on as substitutes towards the end of the Premier League game at Old Trafford and I actually got the better of him! I nipped the ball away from him a couple of times, and he was supposed to be marking me as I lost him, cut inside and fired in a shot to score the Norwich goal in a 2–1 defeat.

At the time of that match he was just 19 years old and an unpolished gem. He had all the raw attributes to become a world-class player, but at

Cristiano Ronaldo: the most complete all-round modern-day footballer.

that stage (and as you would expect) he wasn't the mature, finished product. He was a work in progress and nowhere near the level that he has achieved at his peak.

He had a great physique for football: six foot two tall, strong, quick. He also had really good technical ability. He was two-footed, very skilful and had plenty of tricks, although they didn't always work for him. The stepovers didn't always lead anywhere, and he was a bit hit and miss. His crossing, for instance, was pretty poor, often overhit or hitting the first defender.

So when I left Old Trafford after that game I would have predicted a bright future for him without being totally confident that he would become a top international footballer.

But the characteristic of Ronaldo that I wouldn't have been able to spot was his ruthless desire to improve and make the most of his talents. In fact I've since learned that the desire had always been there. Leonel Pontes, who was youth coach at Ronaldo's former club Sporting Lisbon, once said 'he always wanted to be the best, the strongest, the one who scored the most goals, did the best dribbles. He was terrible for challenges.'

The years since that match have demonstrated that there are very few in the game so prepared to put in the extra effort to analyse, innovate and improve. That has best been displayed in his innovative approach to taking free kicks. He has pioneered a style of taking them that apparently he learned from playing table tennis. He noticed that if he struck the ball in a certain way the ball reacted so erratically that it was difficult to return; and after extensive practice he successfully repeated the trick when striking a football. The outcome was a shot hit with great pace and topspin so that it dipped rather than curved laterally.

The unique speed and dipping effect that he is close to perfecting is caused by a variety of techniques. He strikes the ball using half of his instep and half of the inside part of his foot, and he hits towards the top of the ball, at the valve, which sends air rushing through the ball, altering its movement in the air

Ronaldo himself has explained some of this skill without revealing all. 'The secret?' he once said, 'I will not reveal it, for I would be giving a trump card to my opponents. I can state only the success or failure at the moment of taking the free-kick is directly related to the position of the body, the way one runs towards the ball and the way one positions one's feet. At that moment, I think only about which side of the net I'm going to aim for. I look at the ball, I look at the net and I say to myself "take the kick, Ronaldo", then I shoot. Sometimes it ends well, sometimes not so well.'

But there is absolutely no doubt that in addition to the innovation there has been ceaseless hard work. After a sensational, dipping 30-yard free kick against Portsmouth, which left the England goalkeeper rooted to the spot as it flew into the net, Sir Alex Ferguson said: 'I've seen a lot of stuff written about how Cristiano's free-kicks are all to do with the way he places the ball or strikes it on the valve, but the bottom line is the boy practises and practises. He's always out there at the end of training, banging balls in after the session has ended.'

His then teammate Nemanja Vidić added 'He practises free kicks all the time in training and stays behind when everyone else has gone. Not just free kicks, he practises dribbling, crossing, shooting, everything. If you work as hard as he does, you get your rewards.'

I use the quotes from Ferguson and Vidić to underline my point that having talent is nowhere near enough. The greatest players don't become great by accident – and free kicks like the one against Portsmouth don't happen by chance. They happen as a result of hours on the training ground. How often would he have rehearsed that free kick? Probably somewhere between 100 and 1000 times that week in the lead-up to the game. That's a great lesson for a young footballer. If you do want to perfect something then do the same thing again and again, consistently analysing and improving, repeatedly, hour after hour and day after day.

And it isn't just his free kicks that have moved to another level. His crossing has improved beyond recognition, and his stepovers are part of a much more direct approach to creating chances on goal. Indeed, the very fact that he left Manchester United to seek even greater success and improve his game at Real Madrid tells you much about his hunger and desire.

Critics of Ronaldo say he has got an ego and plays for himself. I don't see that. I see pretty much the closest thing to footballing perfection on the planet. I see an imposing physical specimen – tall, lean, toned, super-fit and able to sustain high-intensity runs. I see someone who has a magical right foot and strong left foot, who can play on the wing or up front, who can shoot and is also a threat in the air, who can dribble and finish with ease. And I see someone with a winner's mentality. Sure, he has a strut about him, but that is all part of his on-pitch demeanour, exuding bulletproof confidence.

I would love to have played in the same team as Ronaldo and if I had to choose one player's attributes to steal for myself they would be his. Lionel Messi is a one-off, a genius, probably the best player the world has ever seen – but even he is not as complete an all-round player as the modern-day Cristiano Ronaldo.

KEY MESSAGES

Lifelong learning is an invaluable attribute to have. An openness to change and innovation is critical, as well as the appetite to improve performance.

Gather and analyse information and feedback on potential development areas.

Ninety-nine times out of a hundred the highest performers also work the hardest. They are prepared to graft and make sacrifices to achieve what they want.

LESSON NINE

TAKE PREPARATION
AND RECOVERY SERIOUSLY

This chapter leads on from the previous one because, as I mentioned, the best way I knew to create the ideal state as I entered each new game was to go through a regimented pre-match routine and then follow that with a regimented post-match routine. To me that's a sign of true professionalism. When people talk about the word in a football context they are often talking about cynical attempts to get an unfair edge. The 'professional foul', for example, is a deliberate tactic to prevent an opponent getting into a goalscoring position. I prefer to take a more positive view. When I think of 'professional' I think of the practical application of all the ideas and concepts that I have shared in this book and, above all, the capacity and will to prepare, play and recover from game after game of top-class football so diligently that they always perform on match day. These kinds of players are the best of the best, and I am in awe of them.

I think of the late, much-missed Gary Speed. I played for Northern Ireland against Wales and his record in football tells us a lot about him: 85 appearances for Wales, many as captain; more than 650 other career appearances, including 535 in the Premier League for teams such as Leeds United, Everton, Newcastle United and Bolton Wanderers.

Statistics like that cannot stack up unless you are dedicated and utterly professional for season after season. Everyone who played against him had so much respect for him because he was hard but fair and top quality. He sustained top-class performances game after game.

I also kept an admiring eye on the progress of Frank Lampard. He was in the youth team at West Ham with Rio Ferdinand when I was at Spurs. It was funny because neither Frank nor Rio really stood out. Because they were related to footballers I was expecting them to be better than they were and at the time their names gave them more credibility than their actual playing ability.

To progress from where they were in the youth team to become two of the best players in England, justifying vast sums in the transfer market, could only have been achieved by a huge amount of hard work, dedication and practice. Frank is not the most naturally athletic and he didn't have talent that was out of the ordinary, so he must have worked his socks off every single day in training, as well as having the mental and physical resilience to play 50 to 60 games a season in the top league.

He really has been the best, most consistent goalscoring midfielder in the English Premier League over the last 10 years. He's scored over 190 goals for Chelsea from midfield – more than most strikers – and his all-round play has been international class for so long. Moreover, he's the consummate professional and a ridiculously nice guy, and in my book that counts for a lot. Some seem to be grudging in their respect for the achievements of Frank Lampard. Not me. I think he's a complete role model.

People like Speed and Lampard are gold nuggets, managers' dreams. Managers don't want players who are a man of the match superhero one week and a complete waste of space the next. They want performers in their team who have the stamina and endurance to sustain consistently high levels of performance and motivation for 45 games and more each season, for year after year. Reading those words is easy enough but actually doing it is unbelievably difficult. Only special athletes are able to achieve this, and they inevitably become the kind of role models that the rest of us lesser mortals aspire to.

How do they do it? I have no doubt that the foundation is world-class preparation and recovery from games.

The good news is that I think that this is achievable for all footballers, regardless of their talent and whether they play at professional, amateur or recreational level. There is really no excuse anymore. The guy who plays in a pub team can prepare in just the same way as someone in the Premier League, not least because the knowledge that he needs is readily available via the Internet and other resources.

Football is an entirely results-driven business, as many rueful managers will tell you. It only really matters what happens during those 90 minutes. So the pre-match and post-match activities are done with a simple aim in mind – to ensure that when the next match day arrives each footballer in the squad is in peak condition, physically and mentally. If they are, then the team has a better chance of playing well and winning. In boxing they say that fights are generally won or lost before the boxers actually get in the ring.

As I matured so did my approach to preparation and recovery. My routine at 18 was totally different to what I was doing in my thirties. As my experience and knowledge increased I found out what worked best for me and I applied new ideas, layer upon layer, until, by the end of my career, I had a pretty detailed and regimented approach that I followed religiously before and after each match. In professional football the games come thick and fast, so it became not so much a routine as a lifestyle. Everything I was doing was trying to prepare for the next game in the best way possible.

My motive for logging my personal regime in this chapter is not to suggest that anyone should follow it – although obviously I strongly believe in the benefits it gave me – but to suggest that each footballer should define and implement their own version if they want to play at their best, whether that be for a Premier League clash or a Sunday morning game on the local park.

We're all different and what worked for me may not work for everyone. The key thing is to have something consistent in place rather than just follow the whims of that day because there's no doubt that for all footballers, at every level and age, the more professional elements that you incorporate into your game the better. Each one only provides a fractional benefit, but those 1 per cents keep adding up, helping you to leave others behind.

In fact, that was the philosophy behind the approach taken by Sir Clive Woodward with the England rugby team in the build-up to winning the World Cup in 2003. He kept finding new areas that hadn't been explored and improved his players by fractional amounts in training. Once he implemented several of these then the improvement on the pitch was noticeable.

More recently, Dave Brailsford adopted a similar approach to drive Team GB's cycling success at the Summer Olympics. Brailsford was the performance director and led the way in transforming what was previously a minority sport into the mainstream by focusing on what he calls 'marginal gains'. This included a scientific dissection to define opportunities for implementing small improvements that would benefit performance on the track. The impressive medal haul of the cyclists highlights what a great job he did.

So this isn't just me shooting from the hip; this is well-established best practice that is promoted by sports scientists and followed by the majority of professional athletes. It's just about having some simple activities and techniques that give you a better chance of preparing for the game, playing in the game and recovering from the game. So let's look at my end-of-career routines and see what you think.

Kick-off countdown

Timeframe	Activity
Six days before kick off	Apart from a few lapses in the middle of my career, for me alcohol was not even on the radar. Alcohol stays in your system for a few days and can have a really detrimental effect on your body's ability to perform. So I might have a few drinks after a game on a Saturday if we weren't playing until the following weekend, but not if I had a midweek game.
Two days before kick off	At this stage I'd start loading my body with carbohydrates such as rice and pasta. That helped my muscle and energy stores to be primed.
Day before match day	I started thinking about the match the day before. Normally we had a lighter training session of around 45 minutes rather than the normal two and a half hours, and we'd go through the opposition and practise set pieces. At this stage the manager might tell you if you are in the team. They tend to have different approaches. Nigel Worthington, for instance, used to tell us the team the day before the match whereas Paul Lambert did so only just before kick off. After training my thoughts tended to drift towards the game: who I'd be up against, their strengths and weaknesses, my role in the team and what I was looking to achieve. But the excitement hadn't started to build at this stage.
Night before match day	The actual routine depends on whether you are playing at home or away. For an away game you will probably travel down that afternoon and then stay in a hotel. As usual I would be drinking plenty of water – which I always did – hydrating up for the game. The average office worker needs two litres a day, so an active footballer probably needs five litres. I was also pretty meticulous over what I was eating. Some of my teammates preferred cake, chocolate or a bag of sweets, washed down by fizzy drinks or a can of Red Bull. Amazing. I wondered if they really knew what that was doing to their body. In the evening some went for a coffee or to the cinema; I just used to chill out in my hotel bedroom, getting physically and mentally prepared. Usually I listened to a Paul McKenna hypnosis tape, headphones on, which I found relaxing and confidence-building. I almost used to go into a trance. He was giving me affirmations and telling me what a good player I was. The tape used to help me get a full and deep night's sleep. In contrast, some teammates used to stay up until two or three in the morning watching television or videos on their laptop and playing computer games. I never understood that. Why would they expect to be able to play well the next day?

Timeframe	Activity
Match day morning	I always started my match day with yoga. Sometimes other players moaned about sleeping in hotel beds and how they woke up with aches and pains. But by the time I came down for breakfast, a yoga session had made me feel flexible and stretched out. Breakfast was just cereal and toast, topping up the carbs for the exertions ahead.
Pre-match lunchtime	Twenty years ago, when I was coming into football, I used to have omelette and chips for my pre-match meal because that's what the club used to give me. Now, that is recognised as being one of the worst possible meals. More carb loading with rice and pasta is the current fashion but that may change.
Hour before kick off	The general perception of the public seems to be that teams get the benefit of an up-and-at-'em motivational speech from the manager just before kick off. The year we got promoted from the Championship, and for some of the next season in the Premiership, Nigel Worthington played a speech from the film *Any Given Sunday*, which is delivered by Al Pacino and is called 'inch by inch'. It's a great speech, one that makes the hairs stand up on the back of your neck. The danger with that, as we saw in the previous chapter, is that you can send players out of the dressing room who are emotionally over the top. They have intensity but no control. Equally it's not a good sign if a manager consistently feels the need to gee up a team before a game. In truth they shouldn't need it. Most managers go around talking to the players quietly, giving them confidence and encouragement. From my perspective I don't think the words of a manager made much difference. It was all down to me and my personal drive and enthusiasm to do well for the team and myself. Either way it actually doesn't matter how you get there as long as you go on to the pitch in the right state of mind, feeling 100 per cent, expecting to play well and win.
Last minutes before kick off	Finally, last thing in the dressing room, I'd use my physical anchor – squeezing my thumb against my forefinger for a couple of seconds – to generate an emotional feeling that goes with the visualisation that I'd done. I found I needed to put a bubble around myself to focus and concentrate on my performance, whereas some are much louder and pumped up. Head down, eyes closed, I completed my preparation. I felt prepared and ready to play, confident, knowing I'd done everything I could. All that was left was that buzz of walking through the tunnel and on to the pitch.

Timeframe	Activity
Within 30 minutes of the end of the game	First, I got some fluids inside me because my hydration levels were low. My personal rule was that I drank water before a game, briefly had some salty and sugary drinks straight after the game to replace the lost electrolytes and nutrients, and then went back to water. I work on the principle that because the body is 75 per cent water it must be a decent choice of drink.
	Although I often felt exhausted after the game and felt the need to rest, it should be a frenetic time for beginning the physical recovery process. It starts with sitting in an ice bath for around three minutes. In hard training sessions and matches you are constantly ripping fibres and the lactate builds in your lower legs. The cold gets the blood circulating faster as well as soothing aches and knocks.
	When I started my career there were no ice baths at all; by the end we were doing it every day after training as well as after games. I have to say that they take some getting used to. Again, it's a mental thing. It's just cold water against your skin. Some people scream while some people sit down and don't bat an eyelid. It took me a while but after a couple of weeks I got used to it.
	After that comes putting on 'skins', which are leggings that constrict your legs. There is a slight pulsating effect that prevents the build-up of lactic acid and forces the blood back up to the heart to reoxygenate it more quickly.
	Then comes food. Sports scientists know the 30 minutes after the end of a game as the 'golden half-hour'. In that period your body's food stores are seriously depleted and you are in starvation mode, so you need to replenish it. What a change there has been to taking in food. It was only in the last two years of my career that we were given food in the dressing room. In the first 15 years you would have food on the bus going home after an away game. If you played at home it might be two hours before you got home and ate. Now players get pasta and lasagne and eat before meeting their families in the players' lounge.

Timeframe	Activity
Evening after the game	As I've mentioned previously, at the start of my career I used to struggle to wind down after a match. In particular, I'd take all the bad points with me into the evening and grow stressed and frustrated as I dwelled on the things that I (or we) could have done better.
	Like many other professionals I often found sleep a problem, either buoyed by the buzz of victory or beating myself up after a defeat. Paul Lambert told me that as a player he found himself still awake at three or four the next morning. In addition, as the night wears on and the adrenalin subsides, the knocks that have you have taken during the game become apparent.
	As I matured I decided that existing in my own little post-match bubble of misery and self-pity was a bit pointless, a bit childish, not desperately enjoyable and, above all, not that helpful. Instead I took the view that as long as I'd done all that I could have done then regardless of the outcome I might as well move on and forget about it. I got to the stage where I left the emotions of the game, regardless of victory or defeat and whether I had played well or poorly, in the dressing room. That enabled me to enjoy the evening, sleep better that night and turn my attention to the next match. That's what the best players do. When the games come so quickly, the quicker you move on the better.
Day after the game	When I was at Spurs in the late 1990s we had a manager called Christian Gross who brought the players in the day after a game. This caused chaos and serious hissy fits. The culture in football is that you play on the Saturday and everyone has a day off on the Sunday.
	But he brought the players in on a Sunday for a jog, a stretch and a warm down, and gave them Monday off. It just shows how people struggle to adapt to change, because all the players were cursing him and swearing about him. Yet later in my career it became the norm.
	The day after a game you tend to be stiff and the quicker you come in, have a massage, get rid of the lactic acid and get back to 100 per cent the better. We were ignorant of this at the time. Christian Gross was way ahead of English football, and I don't think that's the only time that European football has led the way in terms of the science and culture of the game.

By the end of that process I had physically and emotionally recovered from the game and was ready to start preparing for the next one. Those routines allowed me to get myself psychologically right so that I knew that whenever I went onto a football pitch I would probably feel in tune with myself and as prepared as humanly possible.

Many of the techniques are simply common sense, but the problem with common sense is that it's not that common! It's hypothetical, but I believe that if I had not taken preparation and recovery so seriously it would have had a massive impact on my performance. As an example, just think about hydration. Research tells us that a dehydrated body loses between 7 and 60 per cent of its ability to perform – when you consider that the margins between teams are so small it seems crazy for a footballer not to do anything that might give themselves and their team an advantage. It's all about working smarter rather than harder.

ROLE MODEL

Most of the top sportsmen and women in the 21st century are dedicated and professional. As standards have improved those who don't prepare or recover properly really struggle to compete with those who do. So there are plenty of potential role models to follow.

I've had plenty to do with the likes of Russell Martin and Jonny Howson at Norwich City – genuinely dedicated young men who focus all their energies into performing on the pitch. I am full of admiration for them, not least because I know that I would find it a real challenge to maintain that degree of personal discipline.

At international level I know that Phil Jones is highly rated for his dedication. When he was at Blackburn Rovers his manager was Sam Allardyce, and he waxed lyrical about his high standards and strong work ethic. But I'm inclined to look towards the Etihad Stadium and Manchester City for role models. Joe Hart is clearly outstanding in the way he prepares, but for me his teammate James Milner represents the ideal in how make the most of God-given talents.

I've never come across anyone so young who is as devoted to playing at his best, and of course he has already received rich rewards for his efforts. He is playing at the highest level in the domestic and European game, and has represented his country in both the World Cup and the European Championships.

James Milner: a dedicated professional who makes the most of his considerable talent.

I think it is fair to say that there are many footballers out there who have been blessed with greater genetic gifts, but as I've said several times, having talent is nowhere near enough. Milner is also super-smart and has got a great attitude. Apparently this was evident even when he was at school in Leeds. He came away from his education with 11 GCSEs and was equally as strong in mathematics, art and science as he was at the more physical pursuits such as cross-country running, sprinting and cricket. And it wasn't just his academic brain and sporting prowess that impressed.

Recently one of his old teachers said 'I'd have loved James to stay on and do A levels. He was extremely able but I accept his football is taking him a little further than maths might have done . . . James is still exactly the same really nice, calm, quiet, totally unassuming, popular lad he was at school but I always thought that, inside, he had the sort of controlled aggression that takes people to the very top.'

That inner drive propelled him into the Leeds United first team at the age of 16, and Glenn Roeder, one of his managers during his time at Newcastle United, said of him, 'James really is Mr Perfect, he's an A-star person. He said "no thanks" to Newcastle's brat pack. James can seem a goody two shoes but he deserves every bit of success going. Unlike the vast majority of professional footballers he works to his maximum and extracts every last ounce of ability. Most professional footballers, England internationals included, know they could have worked harder and been better but not James. Frank Lampard is the only other player I've managed who does as much extra training.'

I could go on with more references and compliments. Milner is clearly not the norm. He is undoubtedly a perfectionist and doesn't want to be distracted from training and playing. If that dedication involves turning down lucrative commercial opportunities and the lure of nightclubs then that is a price he is willing to pay. So he is teetotal, shuns the social side and trappings of celebrity, and is much more comfortable in the gym than a nightclub. In fact he reminds me of the Olympians who took part in the London 2012 games. You just sense that for him it is all about being the best he can. He's in it for the sport and the competition. Indeed, he illuminates the whole ethos of this book. Because his standards of professionalism are so high he highlights the bad habits of the stupid footballers, the ones with a bad attitude who will inevitably fall by the wayside quicker than they ever have before.

In contrast I predict that because Milner is intelligent and willing to make the necessary sacrifices to make the most of a very decent amount of natural talent, he will continue to sustain a career at the highest level. I wouldn't be at all surprised if he ultimately becomes one of England's most capped players.

KEY MESSAGES

In football there is the opportunity for a Sunday league player to prepare and recover in exactly the same way as a Premiership footballer – it just requires knowledge and commitment.

It is a cliché to say 'if you fail to prepare, then prepare to fail', but it is also accurate. Even small differences in the approach to preparation and recovery can have big implications on performance levels. We all have the opportunity to consider how we can make marginal gains.

Each individual will develop their own approach to preparation and recovery. With practice, new activities can be added that are tailored to our needs and allow us to become more professional and effective.

AWARENESS AND TRANSITION – UNDERSTAND THE REALITIES OF LIFE AS A PROFESSIONAL FOOTBALLER

As my career developed I came to the conclusion that in almost every profession, indeed in life itself, there is a skill required that is rarely talked about. It's simply being aware and prepared for what you will be faced with next.

At the risk of using an overworked phrase, it is true that most of us follow a professional and/or personal journey – let's call it a pathway – where we will inevitably encounter bumps in the road, challenges, difficulties and opportunities. To some extent our success is dependent on how well we deal with them, as I outlined in Lesson Eight. Of course, many people set off in one direction and then change their minds.

I think the first element of the skill that I mentioned is to be crystal clear in your understanding of why you want to travel down your chosen path and the associated benefits and downsides of doing so. The second skill is being aware of what you will encounter along the way. That's really useful knowledge to have because it allows you to plan and prepare yourself for the changes in direction, transitioning smoothly.

Transition is a part of football, business and life; the quicker you transition the more you will prosper. On the pitch Barcelona have the quickest time of any team in transitioning from having the ball to not having the ball; from attack to defence and back again. On the rare occasions that they turn over possession they swarm around the opposition, pressing to get the ball back for five seconds or so. When they do get the ball back they break with startling speed and skill. Only if they haven't won the ball back during that period do they fall into a defensive formation.

Off the pitch I would argue that that kind of quick transition is even more important – both in being aware of and preparing for what is coming and then having the adaptability to prosper once it arrives. So over the next few pages I have outlined a personal view of the realities of life as a pro. I've split this into two. First, I've detailed the benefits and drawbacks. Second, I've mapped out a typical career path.

The realities of life for everyone who plays professional football, both in England and beyond, over a period of 10 years or more are much the same: similar benefits, similar drawbacks, similar career path. I would be astonished if the following reflections on my own experiences do not strike a chord with other pros who also enjoyed a lengthy career. Equally, I would be astonished if anyone just starting their own footballing journey wouldn't be able to look back when they hang up their boots and find some common ground. To have access to this knowledge now rather than looking back in hindsight should be golden information to help tomorrow's professional footballers prepare for their future.

THE BENEFITS OF BEING A PROFESSIONAL FOOTBALLER

1 Being paid to do something that you love to do

You play on the streets, at school and with your mates for free – and when you get the chance to do it every day in a professional environment with top-class players then you have to pinch yourself that you are actually getting paid. I loved every second of both the training and games.

2 Scoring goals in big games

It's just such a buzz that very few people get the chance to experience. To score a last-minute winner gives you a feeling of euphoria that's hard to describe.

Of my goals the one that I remember most fondly is the one in the Championship Play-Off semi-final against Wolves at Carrow Road. It put us into a 2–1 lead with not much of the game to go. The feeling was so intense that I was screaming rather than celebrating.

3 Experiences and memories that you accumulate on and off the field

In addition to the great memories you take from matches there are memories from the lifestyle and trappings you get to enjoy. My favourite memory is the night we got promoted as champions on a night when we didn't even play. I phoned up the whole squad, about 25 or 26 players, and invited them round to my house for an impromptu promotion party. It was a night I'll never forget and a memory you couldn't buy.

I also think about the off-season holidays that I spent in Las Vegas. It became a bit of a tradition at Norwich that a group of players would fly over – first-class of course – and stay in the penthouse at the Bellagio. As you can imagine we had a fair bit of fun and it provided a great release from the intensity of the football season.

4 Enjoyment of playing football with your mates

There's so much laughter every day in training. Yes, there's hard work, but there is also so much fun and enjoyment, particularly when you get a group of lads that get on. I used to almost feel a bit guilty that I was actually getting paid. My old coach at Norwich, Steve Foley, used to say 'have a laugh in training but don't make training a laugh'. Footballers are so witty, everyone's always looking to make a fool out of someone else or make a joke at their expense. When you see footballers interviewed after games they shut down and are straight-laced, but these guys are really witty and humorous away from the camera.

5 Material benefits

I didn't get into football for the money; however, you do get paid well above the average wage and sometimes I was earning more in a month than other people earn in a year. Other professions may deserve it more but, rightly or wrongly, if someone offers you money you are not going to turn it down and it gives you a very, very nice lifestyle. Whether you enjoy nice cars, living in a nice house, buying watches or going on holidays, the money from playing football gives you different options.

DRAWBACKS OF BEING A PROFESSIONAL FOOTBALLER

1 Leaving your family and friends

When I left my friends and family at the age of 16, I didn't realise the significance of what I was doing. For at least six months I was homesick and it was a big wrench, but eventually I got used to it. I didn't realise I would never live in my parents' house again, but over the years that's how it worked out.

2 Social sacrifices

Social sacrifices need to be made if you want to have a successful professional career. There were so many times when my family worked themselves around me. For instance both my brother and sister chose their wedding days around when I could be there. I missed the weddings of at least 10 really close friends and numerous other social occasions. In the social sense my Friday nights didn't exist for 20 years. I would be in bed at 10.30 with a cup of tea. Sometimes, there would be no weekend socialising and that was just part and parcel of the realities of being a professional.

3 The strain you put your body through

Because the games are so physical and you cover so much mileage your body suffers. In addition you are getting kicked and battered. It's a ferocious game with bumps and bruises and it hurts to get up the next morning after a dead leg. In addition to the strain from each match there is the accumulated effect over a career. Some former professionals really do struggle to get out of bed each morning because their body has become close to arthritic. That's another reason why you get paid well while you are playing.

4 The cut-throat nature of football

This is something that a lot of fans don't see. At any time the manager can call you in and say 'I don't want you any more, see ya'. Contracts give you a bit of security but, generally, if the manager decides he doesn't want you any more than that's the end of your time at the club. Either you won't play any more football or he'll make your life a misery by making you train by yourself or doing whatever he can do to get you out of the club as quickly as possible. It can be that cut-throat – and of course these decisions at the club have huge consequences for your personal life. The manager only cares for you if you're performing for him. In truth it's a case of 'give me what I need or see you later'.

5 Insecurity of not knowing where you'll be

There are no jobs for life anymore, but in football most contracts are only one, two or three years in length. So if you only get a one-year contract with a club across the other side of the country, you have to decide whether to move, buy a house or rent a house. And do you sell the house you were living in?

It's that insecurity of not knowing what the future holds. In other professions some people might have the luxury of deciding that they will stay in a certain location and find a job that suits them, whereas a footballer playing in the north who is bought by another club at the other end of the country has little choice but to leave. So, within days, their circle of friends goes and they have to start getting used to a new area. The whole house of cards tumbles, and that's doubly difficult if they have children in school.

The other aspect that I mentioned is the career path and in particular the need to cope with the inevitable transition from one phase to another. Because the careers of long-term professional footballers tend to follow a typical path – barring injuries – they're possible to map out, and here's my take.

CAREER PATH OF A PROFESSIONAL FOOTBALLER

Foundation

These are the pure, early stages of development when football is just about fun and the learning is unstructured and unconscious. This stage ends more quickly now as youngsters with something about them soon become involved with clubs and teams.

My foundation phase took place in Belfast where there wasn't much else to do. We kicked around a ball either in the street or at school at break time, at lunchtime, and in the evenings after homework. I loved it and developed a deep affection for the game that is deep rooted and will never leave me. I also developed a desire to play football for a living over the water in England.

Discovery

As I began to play in formal teams, I excelled, and the word went out that Paul McVeigh had a talent that was worth a look. That led to the discovery phase of my career: when scouts from professional clubs first showed an interest. This was flattering, and for me to travel from Northern Ireland to London and Tottenham Hotspur at the age of 11 was an inspirational moment in my young life.

By now our aspiring footballer will have begun to specialise in a favoured position on the field and establish an identity and self-image as a player. Defender or striker? Creator or aggressor? About now he will be finding himself, helped by mentors and role models who can be critical at this stage (and thereafter) to provide guidance and experience, signposting the challenges ahead. Most high-performing sportsmen enjoy helpful and supportive influences around them, and it is so important that I have devoted a whole chapter to it (see Lesson Eleven, page 127).

Novice

To get to this stage our young footballer has shown a natural talent that has made him stand out. But once he starts playing for a professional club in their youth team he will be at just the same level as the others. At this stage there is a lot of direction and coaching as the football becomes more serious and competitive.

There is also the first real opportunity to tap into the support staff that operates at the club. When I started this wasn't the case. When I arrived at Spurs, one of the biggest and richest clubs in the country, we had just two youth team coaches and a physio to cover the entire squad. Nowadays the bigger clubs have vast arrays of backroom staff, probably 20 just for the youth team. At most Premier League clubs there will be three physios, two or three masseurs, at least one sports scientist, a nutritionist, a chef/dietician, as well as analysts reviewing pro-zone and a strength and conditioning coach. At some clubs they have specialist attacking and defensive coaches. At the higher levels this trend is gathering pace because of the recent introduction of the Elite Player Performance Plan (EPPP), which is a long-term strategy designed to take Premier League youth development to another level. The EPPP is revolutionising football and driving the clubs forward. The focus on youth development has never been more urgent and intense than it is now, and fundamental to that is the creation of teams of expert support staff at the participating clubs.

One of the things that I explain to young players when I mentor them is that although they might have great football potential their knowledge base is very, very low. So I encourage them to gather as much knowledge from the support staff as they can, bearing in mind that these are university graduates from Oxford, Cambridge, Loughborough and the like. These are some of the smartest people, armed with degrees, masters and doctorates, so why wouldn't a youngster pummel them with questions: What do I need to do? How can I improve? Why does this keep happening? For me it is all about getting into a daily routine that helps them achieve the results that they want – and these people can help them along the way because their knowledge is streets ahead.

But in my experience that simply does not happen. In fact it is completely the opposite. I think that they just don't use the support staff at all, or 99 per cent of them don't use them, because there is a culture in football that it is uncool to learn. Instead the young footballers typically adopt the role of children and, as a result, see the support staff as parents. The 'parents' encourage the 'children' to act upon their guidance and adopt their ideas, but they often don't listen and try to get away with as much as possible. How crazy is that? It's just such a waste. Ideally the youngsters should behave like adults and develop a mature relationship with the support staff, working with them, squeezing as much knowledge out of them as possible to help them perform at their best. But that's not the culture of English football at the moment and I don't expect it to change any time soon.

Anyway, by now the possibility of having a career in football becomes clearer for those who are showing signs that they can make the grade; though, of course, most fall by the wayside for a variety of reasons.

Contracted

Receiving a formal contract and becoming a professional footballer is a great feeling, but the money won't be great for the majority. I remember that after two years in the youth set-up I was thrilled to get a professional contract at Spurs, but I was earning £11,000 a year, which made me the lowest-paid player at the club, on less than some of my mates working in Tesco.

In these early stages effort and graft is not yet rewarded by adulation, bonuses and playing at big stadiums in front of big crowds. And the gap between being a new, apprentice footballer and the team's first 11 feels massive, even insurmountable. Certainly our footballer won't be on the radar of the first-team manager as yet, and because they have moved up a level they will automatically have become one of the least capable contracted players at the club.

In coping with these new challenges they will not have the benefit of previous routines. After the regimented direction and structure of the youth set-up, once they turn professional and start playing for the reserves (or the under-21s for clubs participating in the EPPP) they will tend to be left to their own devices.

These can be particularly dangerous times because they will have a small degree of status and new distractions. Furthermore they may be away from home, living in rented accommodation or in a new house away from their friends and family. It is no coincidence that the biggest drop-out rate in football is between the ages of 18 and 21.

They will need to have some maturity, clear goals, a love of the game and take unequivocal responsibility for being as dedicated as they can be.

The gap between signing professional terms and playing for the first team can seem like an eternity, and many get disheartened and disenchanted, hitting a wall and giving up when, in fact, they may have been just a whisker away from the breakthrough. In fact it's a time to get their heads down, work hard and lay the foundations for a long career.

Breakthrough

With hard work and good fortune the breakthrough is made and leads to a first team debut – a day that every professional footballer will remember. Of course, they will experience nerves and anxiety, but it's a real buzz to play in front of a large crowd and often the adrenalin will carry them along. Others will not expect much, so in many ways they have little to lose.

Actually I found it much more difficult after my debut as I tried to establish myself in the team – and I don't think I'm alone in that. Only a small percentage of debutants ultimately play more than 50 games.

Why? Well, there is such a relief to finally make it into the first team and achieve one of your goals that there is certainly a danger that, like me at Tottenham, you go into celebration mode. You've been working towards this for 10 years and now that you've reached the summit of the mountain complacency can set in and it can all go to your head. In fact the hard work is just beginning.

Apart from anything else if you get a run in the first team the expectations of supporters and the manager begin to increase. The debutant is given some leeway, but after 10 or so games the honeymoon period is over. It's time to start delivering.

One additional challenge that can be overlooked is that they will have entered a dressing room and started to mix with a range of ages, personalities and characters. Some of the old pros might be 34 or 35 years old, with their own children. It's important for the player to be able to get on with other people, feel at home in their company and play their part in making sure that the team is just that – rather than a bunch of individuals.

In my early years I was quite shy, and I remember going away with the Northern Ireland national squad and watching the likes of Jim Magilton, Ian Dowie, Neil Lennon, Steve Lomas and Michael Hughes. They were so confident, and just exuded charisma and humour. I wasn't sure whether they were like that because they played football or whether it was just part of their personality. Gradually, though, I felt more able to take part in the banter and ribbing off the pitch, and that helped me to feel more comfortable within the team environment.

It certainly helps massively if the players respect each other (which is quite different to being best mates) and have a connection and camaraderie. In a sporting sense you are going into battle with these guys, and the teams that have a genuine togetherness stand out. Sir Alex Ferguson certainly instils that at Manchester United, and all the late goals Norwich City scored when they got promoted from the Championship were as a direct result of Paul Lambert's ability to construct a group that played for each other.

The Dutch team is a classic example of the alternative: great individual players who consistently underperform because of individual clashes and swollen egos. The team must always come first.

Prime time: proudly in the green and white of Northern Ireland.

With a contract comes the potential of being involved in transfers – and where there's money and deals to be done then you can be sure that agents will be sniffing around. In fact they will have probably been lurking in the shadows for a while if the player has shown a touch of star quality and high potential.

There is no doubt that agents, like them or not, are now a massive part of football at every level. I would say an 18-year-old is unlikely to need an agent unless they are a superstar like Wayne Rooney. Yet many sign on the dotted line. I think what appeals to a lot of young players is that an agent might be able to get them some free boots or onto guest lists at nightclubs. It is so shallow. If a young player wants an agent then they need to get recommendations and find one that is trustworthy and interested in their footballing career

The best players in the world all have an agent. They certainly target talented young teenage footballers in the hope that when they mature they will become valuable assets. In the same way agents build a relationship with a young player coming through because there is every chance that the player is going to use the same agent by the time they mature and start earning decent money.

I have heard stories of agents who have approached young players before they are legally allowed to and buying cars or houses for them or their families. It is an investment for the agent. He is thinking that it might be worth buying a gift of, say, £30,000 for the youngster because in four of five years' time they might be earning £250,000 per annum from the relationship. It's a risk, but there is a lot of investment that goes into young players when there is the possibility that they might go on to make them a lot of money.

The benefits of having a good agent is that they have contacts within the game – with managers, chief executives, secretaries – who are normally the ones who deal with contracts. If an agent has a personal relationship with these people it definitely makes it easier to get the player to that club, assuming that they have worked with the agent before and they respect him and they know that he is going to be straight down the line.

The other benefit of an agent is the fact that they will tend to know the pay structure of a lot of different football clubs. An example: if a young player has made 10 or 15 appearances for a Premier League club but is considering moving to a League One team because he is unable to break into the first team then what can he expect to be paid? The player probably won't know, but the agent will. He will know that the pay structure for a young first-team player in League One might be between £800 and £1500 a week. If the player goes into negotiations expecting twice or three times that amount they're going to be disappointed, but the agent can manage their expectations.

Some agents in my experience are very trustworthy, work really hard, do a good job, help the players out a lot and are not just there for the financial side of it. Gerry Carlile is one example of an agent who has become a trusted adviser and sounding board for his players, someone they can confide in because he understands the ins and outs of football. In the future I hope that other agents follow his example – acting as a mentor, helping players to make the best of their ability.

I haven't met that many of them, but I do know a few like Carlile who are trustworthy, reliable and work really hard on doing a professional job. They also normally stay out of the limelight, which is a decent indication of whether they are a good agent or not.

On the other hand, in my opinion, some agents that I have come across during my career are not trustworthy and do not have the player's best interests at heart. For instance, I wanted to leave a club for the sake of my career. A friend suggested his agent, who he said was 'an absolute shark' but would be able to engineer a move for me. Naively I said that although I didn't agree with the moral side of it I definitely wanted to move. So I signed with him. He did nothing for me for two years. Through my own endeavours, speaking to managers and coaches, I got a trial in Pisa in Italy, and I was actually at the airport on the way over when I got a phone call from my agent. He could hear that I was in an airport or train station and asked where I was. When I told him he said 'you know you are going to have to pay me my percentage if you sign there'. I complained that he had done nothing to deserve it but he said 'look at your contract; it's a worldwide contract. If you sign either they pay me or you pay me or else I will sue you.' That for me was a typical example of how agents work.

Ninety-nine per cent of them just come in, negotiate a contract and take their 5 per cent cut. You might have a few phone calls with them but that is simply because they are trying to keep the relationship bubbling in case it can be of use to them.

Prime time

If all goes to plan then the professional footballer becomes a fixture within the first team. By now they are probably in their peak years physically and beginning to enjoy the financial rewards and recognition. These are the prime-time years: you should relish them and be professional enough to become the best you can be and play as many games of football as possible.

One way to do that is to be versatile. Stupid footballers are resistant to playing in anything other than their preferred position. They have a fixed self-image that leaves little room for flexibility. But they are actually employed as a footballer rather than left-back or centre-forward – so it is logical that the more options they give the manager the more likely they are to get into the team.

Having started my career as a striker I began to get selected on the left wing for Norwich. I preferred to play in the middle but I was open to the change and appreciated the benefits: another string to my bow, all part of the learning curve, more likely to get picked. I still scored goals from there and it gave the manager more attacking options. By the end of my career I had played in every position except centre-half and goalkeeper!

It's also possible to play in pretty much the same area of the pitch but adapt your style. At Tottenham, my former teammate Stephen Clemence adapted his game and made his versatility his strength. He started off as a goal-scoring midfielder. He just kept getting into the box, never came back to defend. That was under Ossie Ardiles. Then Gerry Francis came in and wanted something different so he just used to sit in front of the back four. He never got forward, just sat and played it around like a Ray Wilkins. Then George Graham came in and wanted people ratting around, not really passing the ball too much, and just giving it to the winger. So he turned into a real dogger.

Clemence had that flexibility to morph into three different styles of play – and in doing so he also demonstrated another helpful trait, the ability to adapt to different managers. In all walks of life people need to adapt to new bosses. They all want to make their mark, and in football that need is urgent because time can be limited in such a results-driven and cut-throat business, so they want their players to react positively to their approach and put it into practice. Most teams are a reflection of their manager's personality – the demand for the players is to adapt the way they play to suit them.

I think at this stage of a footballer's life there can be a danger of stagnation, particularly if they have spent a fair amount of time at the same club. When I was 25 I had been at Norwich for four years and I think I got a bit stale and comfortable. That fact, in addition to leaving a long-term relationship, meant that for two years I drank too much, spent too much time in nightclubs when I should have been at home asleep and generally lived like a rock star. Fortunately, although I played hard during that period I worked even harder on the training ground. But there is no doubt that I took my eye off the ball for a while.

Veteran

Towards the end of their twenties and into their thirties our footballer will be at their peak in terms of earning potential, but the contracts that they get offered will become shorter. Many clubs only offer one-year contracts to the over-thirties – a trend that I predict will continue and become more widespread.

Around this stage they will have begun an inevitable physical decline. Of course taking care of themselves can slow that decline, but most footballers have suffered from injuries at some stage and they can accumulate to take their toll.

I remember Gary Mabbutt at Spurs used to have 45 minutes of physio even before training, and extensive strapping applied to his feet, ankles and knees, and even on his chest. Those cumulative aches, pains and hobbles become a burden and are to be avoided, not least because of long-term problems such as arthritis. That said, I have the utmost admiration for Gary, not least because he played top-class football for 20 years despite being diabetic, which is a phenomenal achievement.

On the flipside of the physical decline is the fact that he will have learned how to read a game and have the experience to know what works, both for the team and himself.

Retirement

For many the journey towards retirement can be traumatic. It's all they've known and they are ill equipped for the outside world. The lucky few have the choice of when to retire. Eric Cantona was one who walked away from the game when he reached 30; he knew that he had peaked and didn't want his standards to fall. For others financial considerations must be taken into account. Either way it's always difficult when the cheering stops, and I deal with this aspect in some detail in Lesson Twelve (page 139).

And so the career path, the sporting cycle, ends for our footballer – hopefully to be replaced by new challenges and opportunities. Of course, along the way there are minefields to avoid, bumps in the road to negotiate and there's not a single approach that guarantees success as a professional footballer. However, having openness to change and an awareness of the upcoming new challenges will give you an edge, prepare you for the future and help you get ahead of the game.

ROLE MODEL

Grant Holt is not the most naturally talented footballer. He hasn't got the vision and passing skills of a Xavi, he can't dribble like Messi and he can't strike a free kick like Ronaldo. The players and managers he has worked with will tell you he is one of the worst trainers ever, fans have called him overweight and referees definitely find him a challenge. In his first season in the Premiership he not only won the most free kicks but also conceded the most. Self-effacingly he calls himself 'a big lump'.

That said, you won't ever hear me criticising him because I think he is undervalued. I think he has good technique, is immensely strong and is a top-class finisher – and, above all of that, he is world class in an underrated and little-considered characteristic. I call it *transition*, and by that I mean the priceless ability to adapt and thrive in new circumstances and environments. As we have outlined during this chapter, change is the only constant in football – nothing stays the same for long – and Holt's

Grant Holt: one of the best at relishing change and each new challenge.

ability to deal with each new challenge and flourish has enabled him to carve out a highly successful career.

I can think of few footballers who have had a more varied career, and it's worth a detailed look back on his path through the leagues to appreciate just how far he came to make it into the Premier League.

It certainly started inauspiciously. In his youth he was a defender and was released by his hometown club Carlisle at the age of 16. For a while he played parks football, having switched to centre-forward. He started to hit the net and was spotted by Workington, where he played while he became a tyre fitter.

Halifax, then in the third division of the Football League, showed an interest, but after just one goal there he went on loan to Barrow before the unexpected death of his father put his career on hold.

In 1999 he spent four months in Singapore with Sengkang Marine with the understanding that he would be signed by Carlisle United on his return. But Carlisle entered administration and were unable to complete the transfer so he moved instead to Barrow, playing in the Northern Premier League, where he took a part-time job in a factory in the town.

After two years there Sheffield Wednesday signed him in March 2003. He made 30 appearances, half of them as a substitute, but only managed four goals. He then dropped down to League Two, signing for Rochdale, where he had to wash his own kit between making 83 appearances and banging in an impressive 42 goals.

This led to Nottingham Forest paying £300,000 to secure his services in January 2006. He played 96 times for Forest, sometimes playing out of position during a tense relationship with the club's management. He scored 21 goals and, via a brief spell at Blackpool, went to Shrewsbury, where 28 goals in 51 appearances attracted the interest of Norwich City, who had just been relegated to League One.

He joined in the summer of 2009 – funnily enough, I had my medical at the same time as him – and the rest, as they say, is history. Certainly it has been the most stable and successful period in his career. He has played in League One, the Championship and the Premier League for the club. He became captain and the acknowledged talisman. Throughout he has scored goals. He was top scorer and won Player of the Season in the first three seasons – and he was a whisker away from selection for the English international squad that went to the 2012 European Championships. Not too shabby for a tyre fitter from Carlisle.

They are the cold facts and figures of his rise to prominence, but the key question is how has he done it? How has he managed to silence the doubters who have questioned his ability to cut it each time he stepped up to a new level?

- Could he turn himself from a defender into a centre-forward?
- Could he deal with the difference between Singapore and the north of England?
- Could he make the jump into professional football having kicked around the non-league scene?
- Could he cope with the disappointment of being transferred by Forest and having to drop back down a level?
- Could he score goals in League One for Norwich?
- Could he score goals in the Championship?
- Could he score goals in the Premier League?

Holt has been brilliant at answering each of these questions with a resounding 'yes'. He keeps coming out on top and has shown an ability to keep improving, to keep performing at the next level – not just surviving but also excelling. On a career path, the shorter the plateau at each new level the more you ultimately achieve.

So, for instance, once Holt acclimatised to the Championship he got better and better, and rather than reaching a plateau and settling into a comfort zone his performances were so strong that they indicated he would be able to move up another level, into the Premier League. As it happens he was able to do that with Norwich, but if they had not got promoted I think other clubs would have signed him. Interestingly, the fact that he subsequently put in a transfer request at the club – though he later signed an improved contract – said much about his mindset, his willingness to change and his desire to keep improving.

He displayed those traits when he unselfishly adapted his game to act as a lone striker during much of the 2012/13 season. That may have impacted his return of goals, but showed his versatility.

How has he had done all that? Well, it's all about his mentality. As I've got to know him I've realised that Grant has many of the mental characteristics that I've outlined within this book. He certainly has a strong self-image. He knows what he is capable of and is confident in his own ability, not just to do well at the level he's at, but a level or two above. He has that touch of swagger about him that says 'I deserve to be here'. That's so critical. So many teams go to Old Trafford or the Etihad Stadium and the players are beaten before they've left the team bus. They think they will get beaten and they are proved right. Holt is not like that. In his first season in the Premier League I remember him giving John Terry a real bruising battle. He scored at Stamford Bridge, scored at Anfield and scored against Manchester United at Carrow Road, turning and hitting one into the top corner. You don't do those things on the big stage unless you believe in yourself. Certainly that bit of swagger is so much more helpful then a meek inner voice that doubts whether you can perform.

He also has the strength to deal with adversity and put it behind him. There have been setbacks in his career that would have beaten lesser men – the release by Rochdale, the problems at Forest – but he has showed a real will to succeed, determination and persistence. And he has flexibility in his approach to dealing with new teammates, new managers and coaches, new locations and new levels of football, always finding a way that helps him to always deliver on the pitch. Coping with change is an underrated asset for a footballer – and Holt has proved himself to be world class at that.

KEY MESSAGES

We can all benefit from having an awareness of the benefits and challenges of our likely career path because it provides us with the kind of information that helps us to prepare for new challenges and to transition smoothly from one to another.

Most high performers display flexibility and a positive attitude towards change. They are at a big advantage over those who are resistant.

Transition is a much underrated and often overlooked quality and characteristic.

LESSON ELEVEN

LOOK, LISTEN AND LEARN

When I was 20 years old I was a massive fan of the Italian international striker Gianfranco Zola, who was playing for Chelsea at the time. He took over from Teddy Sheringham as my number one role model. I loved so many aspects of Teddy's game, but Zola shared my body size and shape, and even though I was nowhere near his standard we played in a similar way. Like mine, his game was all about dropping off bigger defenders into holes where he was difficult to mark. He would pick the ball up and link the play with a clever pass or release a shot on goal. Technically he was brilliant, his skills were sublime, and he had exceptional speed of thought and an ability to execute that made him one of the top three best Premiership players ever. He was so far ahead of the game. The much-repeated goal that he scored against Norwich with that cheeky back heel from a corner just summed him up – and that unpredictability was something that I tried to build into my own game.

I became aware that my agent knew Zola and I asked if it was possible for him to try to arrange for me to meet him. He said yes and, much to my delight, so did Zola. So one day after training I drove down to London from Norwich and we went out for lunch. I knew that I would never have the skill levels or natural ability of Zola but I also knew that there was no reason why I couldn't mirror his approach and attitude. So I picked his brains and lapped up his words of advice. He even paid for the lunch!

I sat there with a pen and pad and interviewed him – not with questions about his football career but about the way he prepared and recovered from games. At the time he was about 34 years old but still one of the best players in the league, and I wanted to know how he was still at a peak when most footballers had begun to decline. There wasn't one single jaw-dropping revelation that would instantly transform my career – and nor did I expect there to be – but there was a series of insights into the way that he got the best out of himself that I was able to incorporate into my own approach to help me perform better on match days. Certainly he shared nuggets of information that I found incredibly helpful. He told me that although he based his game on Diego Maradona (with whom he had played at Napoli) he worked much, much harder, including building up his physical strength so that he could hold his own in the tough environment of the Premier League. It became clear that what may have appeared to be instinctive was the result of endless repetition and training ground sweat. He also shared that he was doing tai chi for a couple of hours in the afternoon, something that would be alien to most footballers.

Of course players like Zola are rare. There isn't one like him at every club. Yet there will generally be someone who is respected, experienced and has achieved in the game. As long as they are willing – like Zola – to share that knowledge then they can be invaluable. An experienced player who has played 500 professional games might as well have come out of a university with a first because of his level of experience, knowledge and skills. So my simple advice is to go and talk to that player. The problem is that, as I mentioned in the previous chapter, young players are loath to do this because it's not 'cool'. Since retiring I mentored a centre-midfielder who told me that he wanted to play in the manner and style of an established first-teamer at his club. To me it was so obvious that he should just go and ask him to have a chat and pick his brains – but I don't think he did because he felt uncomfortable asking. There is a definite sheep mentality in the game and too many are scared to be different.

Even if a youngster can't face up to the chilling prospect of sitting down and questioning another footballer they can do the next best thing and watch them, whether that be on the pitch, in the dressing room or on the training ground. Throughout this book I've given many examples of players who caught my eye and I found that if I looked hard enough there was always something to admire that I could integrate into my own routines.

So, for instance, when I was at Tottenham I noticed how Sol Campbell was entirely focused on being the best player he could possibly be. He was getting massaged before and after training every day – the first person I saw doing that – because he saw the benefits. He was ahead of his time. I also picked up on his calmness on the pitch, a quiet composure that helped him to deal with attacks.

Campbell was a great defender. He was a superb physical specimen: a six foot two powerhouse, 15 stone of solid muscle without an ounce of fat on him, and he could run like the wind. I never saw anyone get past him and leave him for dead. I remember playing against him in training. I was quick and nimble and fancied my chances against him. A ball got played up to me and I controlled it, nutmegged him and tried to go round the other side. Really I needed a taxi. He was so big I had to run about 20 yards around the outside.

Another player who I learned from was Darren Huckerby at Norwich. He was a true professional and mentally the toughest footballer I played with or against because he developed this unrelenting, obsessive desire to get fit beyond all normal measurements.

Hucks was a chubby kid but he clearly had the potential to be freakishly athletic because as he began to work at it he became absolutely outstanding over both short and long distances. That's really unusual. The way genetics work means that you generally have fast-twitch fibres or slow-twitch fibres. Those with fast-twitch fibres – stocky, powerful guys – generally become sprinters. Those with slow-twitch fibres – long and thin in physique – are the long-distance runners. But Hucks could do both. In the 10, 50 and 100 metre sprints he was always the fastest – and over three, five and eight mile slogs he was also always out at the front. He just didn't have a weakness. This allowed him to sprint at top speed repeatedly. While everyone else was fatigued after one or two sprints, Hucks just kept going. He was the Duracell bunny.

Some of this was down to genetics but most came through mental toughness, hard work and desire – through being in the gym every day, doing extra work on his speed. After we'd finished training he'd go back in and do a run on the treadmill for half an hour, work on his balance and do extra cardiovascular exercises. So the learning from Hucks was that to improve my speed, strength and fitness I needed to get in the gym and sweat, day after day.

When it came to finishing I watched the clinical Alan Shearer from afar. When we were at Norwich Craig Bellamy would always say that he didn't like or rate him. We'd always defend him and point out his goalscoring record and what he'd achieved in the game. But Bellamy was adamant. 'I don't care', he said, 'he's just a battering ram.' Bellars used to like Romario, Maradona and the creative forwards with touch and flair. Then I spoke to Bellars a couple of years later when they were both at Newcastle and he told us that Shearer was the best and strongest centre-forward he'd ever seen in his life!

Shearer was not particularly tall, certainly not flashy – but he was strong and a world-class finisher. Give him a chance and he'd put it away nine times out of ten. It wasn't until Bellars played with him that he realised just how good he was. He also showed great strength to come back from setbacks, not least two really serious injuries to his cruciate. It's the most serious injury in football. That Shearer recovered and went on to achieve what he did shows the mentality of the man. I learned so much from him without even having a conversation.

I analysed the likes of Campbell, Huckerby and Shearer and adopted aspects of their approach into my own game. At the risk of stating the obvious, that kind of opportunity is there for all. Just switch on the television and watch any game of football and there will at least one player doing something outstanding that you can learn from. Of course that's if your eyes are open to it. I think the key is to be receptive to new ideas and enthusiastic to the possibility of improvement. It's entirely possible to watch but see nothing, just as is possible to hear but not listen.

So there are two immediate ways to improve: watch the best of the best in action and, better still, pick their brains. Another option, which I increasingly employed during my career, was to be 'mentored' by specialists who were not professional footballers. Indeed, I am extremely grateful and indebted to an outstanding group of men who have provided me with support, guidance and advice.

The dictionary definition of a mentor is a 'wise and trusted counsellor'. Personally I see them as a personal satnav – someone who understands the 'journey' you are on and is able to guide you on how to get to your destination; the best direction to take at a crossroads and how to negotiate the bumps and potholes in the road ahead. They are experienced and wise enough to know what is coming and can help you deal with it.

There has been a lot of research undertaken that confirms that most of the high performers in sport have a mentor (or mentors) who helps them along the way. If I think about my mentors I realise they share similar traits, albeit they have helped me in different ways and at different stages of my development.

My dad was my earliest mentor. I picked up so much from him. I totally respected him – and still do – and listened to and acted upon his guidance. He had an incredible determination for me to succeed but in a positive way. He wasn't a pushy parent. He took me to training and encouraged me to give it my all and put in the hard yards. He knew it would be worth it and he was right.

Robbie Walker was also someone I looked up to. He was the scout that I mentioned right at the start of the book who picked me out at that club in Belfast and took me to Tottenham Hotspur. I understood that he knew football inside out, why some young players made it and some fell by the wayside. So I listened to him and lapped up his advice.

Craig Mahoney and Keith Mincher are brilliant sports psychologists and brilliant mentors. I didn't work with them because I had issues or problems. I did so because I knew they could improve my game – and they were certainly influential in helping me to develop my thinking.

Nowadays my mentor is Gavin Drake. Gavin is a specialist in human psychology and constructive thinking. He's also a world-class trainer and coach. Together we have created a company called ThinkPRO (www.think-pro.co.uk) to work with Premier League academies within the EPPP system for the psychological development of young players. I am always picking his brains. He constantly updates me on new ideas and concepts, educating me and helping me to thrive in a new area.

These mentors have some common characteristics and qualities, and I think it's worth documenting these, not least because they may help youngsters find their own mentors. So what qualities do this inspirational group possess?

1 KNOW THE SUBJECT

First, they know their subject inside out. Generally my mentors are specialists in either football or psychology and in some cases both. Their knowledge in those areas is greater than mine, and they are able to act as that satnav that I mentioned as well as educating me and broadening my knowledge.

2 ABLE TO ARTICULATE IDEAS

The best mentors are able to find words that put the concepts and ideas into clear, concise language that I understand. All of my mentors are articulate. They don't waste words and when they speak I listen.

By the way, let me emphasise that this is easier said than done. There are lots of performers who are absolutely brilliant at what they do but have little or no idea of how they do it. So even though someone like Steven Gerrard may be able to spray 70-yard passes without a moment's thought – he just sees the pass and executes it with unerring accuracy – with all due respect, my guess is that if you asked him how he does it from a technical perspective he may struggle to tell you. He just does it. Equally, he turned around the Champions League final in 2005. Liverpool were 3–0 down at half time before Gerrard inspired them to one of the greatest comebacks of the modern era. How did he do that? Would he be able to coach others to do the same? Personally I doubt it. So the greatest performers do not automatically make the best mentors.

3 RAPPORT

With all my mentors I have quickly built a rapport that was the foundation of our relationship. We became more than mentor and mentee – there was friendship and a genuine chemistry. With some people the conversations flow quite naturally, with others it's not so comfortable. I recognise now that this is a key part of the mentor's skill set. They need to help their mentee feel at home and open up.

4 LISTENING SKILLS

All my mentors are great listeners. They assume little; they just let me open up and often I come up with own solutions without them having to actively contribute much. Listening is a much underrated skill.

5 GENUINE INTEREST AND CARE FOR THE SUBJECT

This may be a controversial one, but I believe my mentors genuinely care for me and want me to be successful. I suppose the relationship could be entirely clinical and professional – but I'm not sure that would work so well.

6 TRUST

I certainly feel I can trust my mentors. I could tell them anything, on any subject, and I would be 100 per cent confident that it would go no further. If that trust is ever broken then it cannot be rebuilt, so any sensitive information or gossip must never be shared with others. As a mentor, I assume that everything about the relationship is off limits for others.

7 BE HONEST

There's a saying that only your best friends will tell it to you straight – and my mentors have certainly not been averse to telling it to me straight. Once we had built trust and rapport, and they had listened to what I had to say, they haven't sugar-coated their words, and their direct but constructive guidance is highly beneficial to my development.

8 PROBLEM SOLVING

My mentors have also used their skills to help solve problems. Often they do so by asking the right questions, listening and then leading the conversation in the direction it needs to go.

9 PURPOSE AND STRUCTURE

Linked to problem solving, they ensure the discussions have a purpose. They have not been lovely, warm chats that feel great but go round in circles. There is always a sense of progression and momentum.

So that outlines the common threads that I have been lucky enough to find in my mentors, and if a youngster is fortunate enough to find someone with these kinds of qualities who is willing and able to mentor them then I would urge them to seize the opportunity with both hands.

What's the best time for a mentoring relationship to begin? I see no great value in waiting too long. Anything after 11 years of age would work, and there is certainly no end date because mentoring can take place throughout a whole career and beyond. I am definitely comforted that there is always a trusted ally available to signpost the way ahead and point out the bumps in the road.

Perhaps one of the reasons why I'm so passionate about the need for mentoring is because it's an area that I'm now working in. I love it, mainly because I know I am really making a difference. In football I've pretty much done it all and seen it all. I'm confident that tapping into my broad range of experiences can help a youngster avoid making the same mistakes that I have made and focus them in the right direction.

As I've explained, the trick is not so much to give the right answers but to ask the right questions. Certainly questioning is particularly essential in the early stages of the relationship. I've found that in the first few minutes I can get to know the player best by encouraging them to talk through these kinds of open questions:

- What's your background?
- How do you see yourself?
- What are your strengths and weaknesses?
- What are your goals and ambitions?

I find the answers useful because it helps me understand the way their mind works. I can see into their psyche. In particular, the language they use gives a lot away. I hear and pick up on innocent-sounding words dropped into the conversation. I can also pick up on their tone and their body language to provide clues that help me to decide what questions to ask next. Of course encouraging them to talk also builds up our rapport.

I love the fact that no one chat is the same, although it's inevitable that most involve solving what the player perceives as a problem. A typical example is that they may have a bad game and it's preying on their mind for days after. Or they may have made a mistake in a game and it affected their confidence thereafter. That's where I try to simplify their thinking. I help them to understand that no one is perfect and it's unrealistic to think they can be. I encourage them not to think in terms of 'mistakes' or 'failures'. No player has ever played a perfect game.

I think I have an advantage over, say, parents who haven't operated in big-time sport. Ninety-nine per cent of the time the parent has little or no experience of professional sport and understandably some will be overzealous or overprotective of their child. For instance, they may not understand the culture within the game and the kind of banter that takes place in dressing rooms. So if their child gets some stick then they may not appreciate that it's just part and parcel of the game – as long as it's within the normal boundaries – and not something they need to get concerned about. My job is to make them aware of this. Their intentions are always well directed so it's just a matter of working with them so they can help rather than hinder their child's progress.

You will have noticed that I am a strong advocate of these kinds of relationships so it will be no surprise that my advice to any youngster in any profession is clear: get yourself a mentor! However, I have one caveat to add. It is not a one-sided relationship, and it can only work if both parties are committed. As I've detailed, there are characteristics that mentors require to help make the chats productive, but the young footballer has to have a complementary kind of attitude. If not I'd suggest they don't even bother trying to find a mentor.

1 WILLING TO OPEN UP

Once trust and rapport has been built up then the player needs to open up and be totally honest. There's no point in them saying what they think the mentor wants to hear. They need to tell it how they see it.

2 ENTHUSIASM AND DRIVE

The player needs to be focused and target-driven, with a genuine desire to succeed. I mentored a talented young player every week for a year. He had been top scorer in his youth team, been head boy and earned himself a professional contract, and was training with the reserves and first team. Yet he lacked the desire to commit. Ultimately our mentoring sessions drifted away and I didn't see it as my role to contact him to arrange the next session. Sadly, the football club released him even though his ability was not in doubt.

However, I feel he still has every chance of making it as a long-term career if he is prepared to put the hours in and sacrifice what needs to be done.

3 LIFELONG LEARNING

Finally, the player needs to commit to lifelong learning and have an appetite for new ideas and concepts. I think of nurses and doctors. They need to continually acquire new knowledge and techniques because science is evolving so quickly. Even the top consultants stagnate if they don't keep learning. That's a perfect attitude for a young footballer to take, an ideal mentality – and having a mentor can be a key part of that.

When the kinds of characteristics that I've detailed in this chapter are displayed by mentor and mentee then the relationship is almost certain to become incredibly valuable and will certainly give the player a massive advantage over others.

In summary, I've learned that committing to lifelong learning is a great mindset to have. At first I unconsciously found myself drawn to heroes and role models such as Paul Gascoigne. I wanted to be like them and play like then – which is always a great way to learn. Gradually I consciously seized opportunities to make contact with those I respected and admired, such as Gianfranco Zola. I became much more proactive, keener to seek out new knowledge, not prepared to wait for it to fall into my lap. But perhaps my greatest point of learning was to fully understand the benefits of linking up with mentors. Nowadays I am both a mentor and a mentee, and regardless of my role I always find the relationships stimulating and beneficial.

ROLE MODELS

I was spoilt for choice in finding footballers who have mentors. Although they may not have that particular label attached to them, most professional footballers will be able to point to someone who has been a 'wise and trusted counsellor'. Of course, because of the culture in football it will not necessarily have been a conscious, well-thought-out relationship with a structure to the discussions. More likely it will have just happened, quite instinctively and quite naturally.

In addition there are certainly some high-profile managers who have benefitted from having a mentor. José Mourinho is one. He was part of the support staff employed by the late Sir Bobby Robson when he was manager of Barcelona. Mourinho constantly picked the brains of the elder statesman, and that proved to be a great education and preparation for when Mourinho moved into his own career as a manager. Similarly, Paul Lambert played under the management of Martin O'Neill at Celtic. He is happy to admit that he picked up tips and techniques that have been incorporated into his own ways of working.

Players inevitably receive daily guidance from the support staff and management at their football clubs, but the relationship often works best when the relationship is not built upon an imposed management structure.

There is a vast reservoir of talent and experience at Old Trafford. Players such as Paul Scholes and Ryan Giggs have played at the highest level for many years and know how to prepare for and win games of football like few others. So despite the culture in football that I have mentioned, the young players there would have to be pretty stupid footballers not to take advantage of that vast reservoir of knowledge.

Tom Cleverley seems to be one who is keen to look and learn. He recently said:

> Playing for United and alongside someone like Scholesy is what every young lad dreams of. He is a great mentor for me – I look to him every day in training and he is definitely someone I can learn a lot from. The likes of Scholesy and Giggsy always have a picture in their heads about what they want to do with the ball and their first time passing is second to none. The way they go about training and matches means they are two of the best in the world to learn from.

Wayne Rooney may be younger than Giggs or Scholes, but he also has a glittering track record in domestic, European and international football. So it's astute of Danny Welbeck to want to pick his brains. Welbeck recently said:

> I owe Wayne a lot. He has been a terrific friend and a brilliant help to me. We have really forged a great partnership. And he is amazing during a game. He never stops yapping in my ear, telling me, 'Daniel this' and 'Daniel that'. Wayne's funny like that, he calls me Daniel on the pitch, even though most people call me Danny. Yet off the pitch it's Danny or Welbz. Don't ask me why. I'm so lucky he wants me to do well and is always trying to advise what's best for me.

Danny Welbeck: a smart young footballer and blessed to be developing his approach to the game at Manchester United.

I like the way that Rooney wants to share his knowledge and the way that Welbeck is receptive to receiving it. Welbeck and Cleverley seem to be two who are happy to take advantage of the free support around them. That is smart thinking.

KEY MESSAGES

The scope to learn from others is vast, via role models and mentors – yet many neglect to take up the opportunity.

Mentors can be invaluable in helping us be aware of the path ahead. They are like a personal satnav, and the best mentors have a range of skills and attributes, including specialist knowledge, relevant experience and outstanding communication skills.

Mentoring can only work if we are prepared to engage, listen and take action. If we are not prepared to be open and honest then we shouldn't waste the time of our mentors.

THERE IS LIFE AFTER FOOTBALL

Being a professional footballer was a fulfilling and rewarding experience, but since hanging up my boots I am relishing my life even more. In fact, I would go as far as saying it was the best decision I ever made.

I still have the opportunity to enjoy football through my media duties, but I am more able to enjoy travel, hobbies, music and the other facets of my life. Since retiring I've run a marathon, jumped out of an aeroplane, cycled from Belfast to London, done a bungee jump, fought a professional boxer, written this book, started a company, delivered a regular radio show on BBC, appeared on Sky TV, delivered stand-up comedy, interviewed an Olympic gold medallist (Dani King) in front of 50,000 people and moved to London! Phew.

Being a professional footballer was an amazing experience, but the discipline required restricted me. Christmas is a good example. During my career I always played on Boxing Day so my liquid intake on Christmas Day was confined to orange juice and water. After retiring, having my first beer on Christmas Day was an unbelievable experience. I only had two because I wanted to savour the opportunity to sit at a family party with a drink in my hand and just wallow in watching everyone enjoying themselves.

However, I am confident that in relishing my new lifestyle I am in the minority. Many performers struggle to come to terms with life after their sporting career has finished and there has been a lot of publicity recently on this subject, particularly when it has led to depression.

It is hard to say how much the high-profile cases of depression have been linked to retirement. I don't know enough about mental illness to give an expert opinion on it – because there are obviously physiological, social and psychological aspects to take into account – but I know several former players who have struggled to make the transition, and I would suggest that almost all of them would rather still be playing. Certainly two of my good friends and former teammates at Norwich City, Leon McKenzie and Darren Eadie, suffered difficult times once their playing careers ended. I'm absolutely delighted that they seem to have fought through their personal challenges and bounced back with new interests. But there is a clear contrast here: why am I already enjoying life after football so much when many others find the transition so testing?

First, I think it really helped me that that I decided to retire from football rather than football retiring me. I considered whether I wanted to keep scrapping around for a contract or go out on a high – having been part of the Norwich City squad that were champions of League One and secured promotion to the Championship – and finish on my terms. The answer was that I wanted to take on new challenges and pursue new goals – and that meant that psychologically I was in a better position. I had taken the decision. It was my choice and my responsibility.

I was more fortunate than my former colleague, Dean Ashton, who was a top player but got injured with England and had to retire in his mid-twenties. I think he would admit that it was difficult for him, and he took a while to adjust, develop other interests and rediscover a sense of purpose.

I think one other advantage is that I have always had wider interests, so didn't live entirely in the football bubble. It is very easy to get caught up and there were times during my career when I was more obsessed than I probably should have been or wanted to be. However, I think the majority of the time I've had interests outside of the game.

For example, I used to rent out houses to students so that even when I was playing football I was collecting rent, sorting out the maintenance and contracts, and helping tenants to get settled. In addition I learned to speak Italian and a bit of Spanish, I learned to play the piano and the guitar, and I went salsa dancing with my fiancée. I also did a degree. I wasn't the brightest in school but I always had an idea in my head that I wanted to educate myself, so when I was about 21 I enrolled on a business management degree and went to college about three times a week. At that stage I actually found doing the degree too much of a commitment and too tiring, so I put it on the back burner for a few years, but I remained committed to earning the degree, and later on I completed the course and gained the qualification.

These pursuits gave me variety, some stimulation for my brain and, most importantly, a perspective outside of football and an opportunity to take a break from the relentless intensity between matches. If you are writing an essay for your college work then you can't afford to wallow in self-pity after you've played really badly, and I think that is helpful. If you ask any sports psychologist, coach, manager or player they will tell you that there is little to be gained by wallowing in the misery of defeat or a bad performance. Having other interests refreshes the mind and gives you much greater depth and richness in your life.

In contrast, I find that many footballers are addicted to their Xbox and play on it all day once they have finished training. I'm not judging people, but I would question whether they are using their precious time wisely and whether it is going to help them create the life that they want after football.

Indeed, I feel sure that the reason so many players fall into depression and struggle to deal with the transition of coming out of football is because they only have football-related ambitions and their identity is entirely dependent on others. They just see themselves as a professional footballer and so can only maintain that status if a club offers them a contract. But time always passes, and they eventually become too old, too slow or too fat to warrant a contract. When the contract is gone so is their identity.

I have heard people in the game say 'this is the only thing I know. I don't know what I would do if I wasn't a footballer.' Of course, it doesn't have to be like that. The trick is to begin to think about life after football about 10 years before it begins. Rather than being one of those players who comes out of football and thinks 'OK, now what do I do?', the switched-on ones already know what they want to do, or at least have an idea of what kind of direction they want to go in, and start to put things in place to create their future.

ROLE MODEL

A good example of having a fulfilling life after football is my friend Colin Murdock. Colin started as an apprentice at Manchester United and then his varied career path took him to Preston (where he played more than 200 first-team games), Hibernian, Crewe, Rotherham, Shrewsbury and Accrington Stanley. At the end of the 2008/2009 season he retired from professional football after 17 years and over 400 appearances.

Colin Murdock: 'The Professor', perhaps the brainiest footballer I've played with.

Throughout his career his nickname was 'the professor' because he was brainy and because he read books on the team bus. Normally he was studying. He undertook a law degree and became qualified as a lawyer while he was playing. So, as you imagine, he stood out in the world of professional football. Some of his teammates didn't quite know what to make of him, and he undeniably brought something different and unusual to the clubs that he played for – there are very few players who are so highly intelligent and far-sighted enough to be looking towards life after football while they are still playing.

I knew Colin because we both represented Northern Ireland at international level and I found him a likeable character, another whom I learned from. I was always drawn to those that were different and not stereotypical footballers.

Of course, through his hard work he created opportunities for himself when he decided to retire from professional football. He knew that there would be good prospects within the sport for someone with a law degree and, sure enough, he now has a thriving business. He is the owner of a newly created specialist sports management company called Murdock Sports Management Limited, a registered lawyer with the Football Association and an elected expert panel member of the FA Football Judicial Panel.

That's a pretty high-powered and stimulating way to make a living, and Colin Murdock laid the foundation for that during his footballing career by having the vision to look ahead and prepare for the future.

KEY MESSAGES

We must be careful to ensure that we define our status and self-image rather than being dependent on the views of others.

Having interests outside of our day-to-day profession can help to bring a better perspective on life and ensure that we don't get too caught up in what could feel like a daily grind. Variety really is the spice of life.

Preparation for 'retirement' should start well before the actual moment. Have the foresight to take time, look ahead and plan for the longer term. Think about tomorrow as well as today.

THE FINAL WORD

If you've got this far in reading this book then you will probably have already reached the same conclusion that I have. It's one that is simple and straightforward to relate, and became particularly apparent as I left the day-to-day rituals of preparation/match day/recovery and applied the lessons to my life outside of the game.

My conclusion is this: that all of my lessons may have been collected during a career in sport, but if I had opted for a different profession – a plumber or a postman, a brain surgeon or a barrister – then I would have collected the same ones. With the gift of hindsight I realise that my chosen profession has been irrelevant. Actually, what I have shared here is not just what I have learned about football. It is what I have learned about getting the most from my life.

Football remains a massive passion of mine, and nowadays much of my time is spent mentoring young and senior professionals, as well as keynote speaking and sports presenting (www.paulmcveigh.co.uk). I know that some of you will read this book and feel inspired, and I would defy any player, at any level, to improve their mentality and professionalism in the ways I've set out and not enjoy a tangible improvement in their performance on the pitch. Yet I get exactly the same joy and satisfaction in knowing that this book will help readers in different walks of life.

We are all works in progress and if we want to achieve our goals then the need to graft and improve is never-ending. I've tried to share the concepts in a way that encourages this. I hope you have enjoyed the stories and anecdotes, and I hope it has provided food for thought. Now, I urge you to take action, develop the way you think and reap the inevitable benefits! To paraphrase from my favourite book – I hope that I have awoken the giant within you. Life provides such an abundance of opportunities for fun, fulfilment and achievement. So if you want more of whatever makes you feel good then there is no better time to start to make it happen than now!

I have learned that life is incredibly precious. I have such a passion and enthusiasm for making the most of my life that I am willing to do whatever it takes to create the life that I have taken the time to decide is worthwhile and successful for me. I don't want to get to the end of my days and think 'I wish ...'. So instead of looking back with regrets at the end of my days, I am taking everything I can out of each day, because if I don't have any zest and love for my life then who will? I appreciate the huge amount of beautiful yet simple things that are around me, and so when anybody asks me how I am doing, I say 'embarrassingly well'! The statement 'the world is a terrible place' could be justified if you look for evidence. Likewise, 'the world is an amazing place' could be too. I know which statement I prefer to focus on.

PAUL McVEIGH'S STATISTICS

Born	**6 December, 1977**
Height	**5ft 6in (1.68m)**
Place of birth	**Belfast**
Nationality	**Northern Ireland**

CAREER

Club	League App	League Goals	FA Cup App	FA Cup Goals	League Cup App	League Cup Goals	Other App	Other Goals
Norwich from 23 Jul, 2009 to 31 May, 2010	4 (5)	0	0 (0)	0	0 (0)	0	2 (0)	0
Luton from 1 Aug, 2007 to 23 Jul, 2009	24 (14)	3	3 (2)	0	1 (3)	0	3 (3)	0
Burnley from 22 Mar, 2007 to 7 May, 2007	6 (2)	3	0 (0)	0	0 (0)	0	0 (0)	0
Norwich from 23 Mar, 2000 to 1 Aug, 2007	148 (67)	36	7 (1)	2	3 (5)	0	3 (0)	1
Tottenham from 1 Aug, 1996 to 23 Mar, 2000	2 (1)	1	0 (0)	0	0 (0)	0	0 (0)	0
TOTALS	184 (89)	43	10 (3)	2	4 (8)	0	8 (3)	1

INDEX